Divine Intervention

Janet Freedman

Contents

DEDICATION iv

1 Childhood 1

2 Adolescence.. 24

3 Maryland Institute College of Art...................................... 36

4 Downtown Adventures and Divine 54

5 Addendum – letters and pictures..................................... 167

About the Author 188

OTHER WORKS 189

MY WEBSITE.. 190

  WWW.STUDIOPROSE.COM 190

Endnotes.. 191

DEDICATION

To Stumpi, Mr. Nice, Bonnie Gosdsik (Boom-Boom), GoGo, Kit, Aunt Bea (Divine), Spider Lady, Harriet (Galaxy Gruber), Uncle Paul, Chuck (Smokey the Silver Flash), David Lochary, John Waters, Pat Moran, Bonnie (Mary Vivian) Pearce, Mink Stole, Lee Hoffman, Bob McCormack, Greg, David Lehman, Celeste, Ga-Ga, Miss Mess, and Batty. I dedicate this book to you and in memory of the good times we had in The Marlborough.

There are places I'll remember

All my life though some have changed

Some forever not for better

Some have gone and some remain

All these places have their moments

With lovers and friends I still can recall

Some are dead and some are living

In my life I've loved them all

(Lennon-McCartney)

1 Childhood

I was born into a home of financial caution and religious zeal, in an East Baltimore row house one half block from both St. Matthews church and the garish lights of Luby's Chevrolet. It seems to me now that those buildings represented the contradictory tows of my childhood - the good, delineated by an ever present and ponderous religious life versus the tempting temporal world so flamboyantly illustrated by that car dealership's art-deco signage in flashing pink and turquoise. In pleasant weather and through sticky-hot Baltimore summers, the windows on either side of the church sanctuary would be opened and from my pew, bored sleepy with the drone of sermons and prayers, I could spy the shapes and colors of fanciful Luby's sparkling on the day like a charm.

My parents were devout. From babyhood my brother and I were immersed in Christianity, attending church and Sunday school plus a widening number of activities as we grew. At home we listened to the "Youth for Christ" daily radio program. Our stereo played hymns sung by Tennessee Ernie Ford or Billy Graham's George Beverly Shea. "How Great Thou Art" became the background music of my life. My parents tithed their income, yet often scrimped to make additional contributions to special projects or to meet the church's financial shortfalls, a frequent topic of dinner conversation. My mother became an advocate of missions. Little cardboard coin banks for global mission projects appeared with regularity on our kitchen table and into which we were expected to deposit our pennies. With amazing stamina, she managed a succession of church fundraising projects: bake sales, bazaars, candy sales and dinners, all produced with volunteer labor, including, as I grew, mine. At a young age I was sent door-to-door to solicit orders for bake sales. A timid child, I was uncomfortable ringing the doorbells of strangers; some people were kind, some surly, some doors closed in my face without words. I began to evaluate outcomes by assessing the houses, skipping those with darkened windows or a bare and cheerless stoop, lying to my mother when asked if I had knocked at every door, certain I was committing a grievous sin.

Money - or rather scarcity - was the underlying groundwork of my mother's worldview. She'd been born into a large family on a Chesapeake Bay island, and there'd not been money for any but the most basic of needs, thus through her growing years she had often felt beggared and empty-handed. Her memories contained tales of cautious economies, sparse homemade Christmases and a child's winter coat handed down through six siblings. She received her first toothbrush when a public health nurse distributed them in her third-grade classroom. After attending the local grammar school, she walked a four-mile round trip to Stevensville in order to attend the two-story, four-classroom frame high school from which she graduated in a class of twelve in 1931. She had been an excellent student, but her family had no knowledge of or ability to access further academic opportunities, thus after graduation she took her youthful dreams to Baltimore, bunking with an older brother's family in a tiny apartment while attending secretarial school. I think she saw this as her opportunity to alter life's course, and her father, in support of her hopes, managed to provide the modest tuition dollars. She graduated in 1932 in a city bereft of employment opportunity, her dreams of success blighted by America's Great Depression. Throughout her life she often spoke of the disappointment and fear of that time, remembering the anxiety she'd felt as she laundered her one nice dress and polished her shoes in preparation to set out each day in search of work. Her life experiences left her imprinted by austerity, by a fear of doing without, of not having enough, even when life gave her much more.

My parents met at church. St. Matthew's was three short city blocks from her brother's apartment, and she began attending services at the invitation of another young woman in the neighborhood. My dad's family were established members of the church where he participated in a variety of church activities. He was a sharp dresser, gregarious, friendly, generous, liked by everyone, he stepped more lightly through life than she. My mother was a beautiful woman, though she never truly knew it, always thinking her younger sister was the beauty because of some chance remark their mother made long in the past that still felt like a wound. She justified her critical appraisal of her appearance by offering as evidence the fact that no young men had courted her as they had her sister. "If I stayed on the island", she said "I might be a spinster living with my parents. Or I'd been married off to a waterman or farmer." She said this not with distaste but with disinterest as if a piece of her had always wanted more than what the island offered. It had me wonder later why she could never see nor support that same sort of dream in me.

My dad, like the fathers of most everyone I knew, worked in one of the many factories of blue-collar Baltimore. It seemed to me that we should not have been less prosperous than those with occupations no better and some worse, though they seemed to have more, perhaps, I thought resentfully as I grew older, by putting less in the collection plate.

While shopping for new items was a rarity, our home was chock-full of things - items picked up at the White Elephant table at church bazaars or handed down from my dad's family or a neighbor. Our furnishings were over large, most of them purchased when my

4

parents married in 1937 and now out of style – fat upholstered pieces with squat ornate legs lavished with corded fringe, their arms and backs covered with crocheted antimacassars. A mahogany suite overwhelmed the dining room where the table was cleared for holiday meals but more often it functioned as an office for the church, its surface heaped with files, Sunday school projects and mimeographed newsletters. In the northwest corner of that room, wedged between a large buffet and a coat rack, a folding table held the current money-making projects for the church – boxes of *Mary Sue* and *Naron* Easter eggs, bags of Christmas candies, china plates with gaudy gilded edges and an image of our church in the center, bookmarks, bibles and an assortment of homemade doodads. In our front hall a reproduction of Sallman's "Head of Christ" was displayed in a three-way lighted frame draped with palm fronds. Our home abounded with East Baltimore kitsch, crocheted crosses and towel holders, and plastic placemats worthy of a John Waters movie set. In my mother's defense, the house had little storage space; in criticism, her propensity to hold onto old or unused objects rendered our space perpetually over full. Our basement eventually became the catchall space for numberless things being saved "just in case". The terror of the Depression never left her.

My mother's frugality and capacity for work was remarkable. She canned much of our winter food supply, sewed and patched our clothing, made dish towels out of flour sacking, and produced unappealing soap from rendered animal fat and lye. A small, crocheted turtle in our bathtub held barbed splinters of soap, allowing every bit to be used before starting a fresh bar. Leftovers from meals, no matter how small the portions, were saved. If not eaten promptly, I was charged with carrying them to Mrs. Otto, a widow who lived on our street - two meatballs, a portion of stew, a withered chicken leg. Although Mrs. Otto seemed pleased to receive them, I was embarrassed, even at a tender age, to be bearing such poor gifts. Mrs. Otto collected newspapers and cardboard for resale and did sewing and laundry for many of our neighbors. Her small, cemented backyard sprouted rows of pronged wooden frames on which she stretched lace curtains and tablecloths to bleach and dry in the sun. Everyone was shocked when upon Mrs. Otto's death, her son and sister found so much money in her house that they had to carry it to the bank in shopping bags. She had the same disease as my mother.

I expect that my mother's frugality brought her a sense of safety. Her cautions, sprouting as they must have from past austerity, existed both as a protection and a warning. In later years, when I commented on her propensity to save old and worn items, she would point out that my post World War II world was a bountiful one. "You only know good times" she said, "but don't think it can't happen again."

I think that her behaviors also rose from a desire to do things as right as she knew how to do them, to achieve some level of envisioned perfection, to have a life neatly arranged to fit some adopted rigid standard. I think it made her serious and harder than she meant to be. But the messages I absorbed were clear: Disaster looms. Be cautious. Follow the rules. The world is not safe. And there will never be enough.

******

I do not suggest that my brother and I were unloved, for we were indeed loved, both by our parents and within the broader family. The breach for me was in my relationship with my mother, a gulf that widened as I grew. I loved her - at times adored her, completely in awe of her strength and all-knowingness, but also discouraged by her frequent criticism of me. While she spoke with pride of my brother's accomplishments, her repeated mention of my shortcomings convinced me that I had fallen short of expectations and was not the daughter she might have wished for. Given the evidence I could not blame her. My brother Gary was an excellent student and achieved grades that earned him entrance to the prestigious engineering program at Baltimore Polytechnic Institute. I, on the other hand, failed at memorizing the multiplication tables in third grade and in high school struggled to attain a passing grade in shorthand. I mucked along at school, finding it mostly mind-numbing and tedious, and though I wanted to do well, I often felt lost as to what the point of it all was. This was likely a worry for my mother and the source of her criticism. I imagine her aim was to put me on some path she considered "right", and it grew out of a concern for my future in what she considered to be a harsh world.

The message I absorbed was that I should be some way that at my core I was not, and it was not alright to be the way I was.

My sense of daily life in childhood is one of sluggish, structured time, filled with the drone of church activities, schoolwork and chores, but interspersed with red-letter pleasures. There were holiday celebrations, visits with extended family, trips to the library and the walk home afterward with books piled to my chin, awash in the sweet anticipation of reading time. On visits to the homes of relatives in two rural locations, I discovered a blossoming pleasure in the colors and intricacies of nature. The items that charmed me were often small: tiny wildflowers, patterns in leaves and tree bark, the swaying grass of a salt marsh, the delicate ridges left on a sandbar by a retreating tide. This variety of color, shape, texture and pattern were a constant source of delight and would one day become a central focus of my artwork. Generally, however, my life seemed overcast, diminished by my longing to do things well and my anxiety over how frequently I did not fulfill expectations. Teacher comments on elementary school report cards describe me as a cheerful cooperative child who is subdued in class, reads well and sometimes produces messy papers. As early as kindergarten a teacher noted on my report card: "She seems to take a passive rather than an active part in class discussions and does not talk as much as do other children" to which my mother replied "I cannot understand why she doesn't take an active part in class. She has lived in a land of 'make believe' since she was 2 years old." While "make believe" was surely a failing in my mother's eyes, research describes it as a completely natural phase, starting at the age of 18-24 months and continuing to approximately 5-6 years.

More recently I stumbled upon the work of Elaine N. Aron, PhD and through her a number of psychologists and therapists whose work focuses on "HSPs" - Highly Sensitive Persons. It is thought that the traits of an HSP are genetically inherited, but their manifestation may be a result of both genetics and environment. Dr. Jerome Kagan, a psychologist at Harvard University, spent much of his career studying babies and the marked differences in temperament between those classified as highly sensitive (or shy, timid), and those who were more outgoing and less inhibited. It is now thought that 15 – 20% of the U.S. population is HSP, representing over 50 million people. My initial reaction was to dismiss the HSP research as nonsense, but in Dr. Aron's book entitled The Highly Sensitive Person, she provides a self-test of twenty-three questions and I was startled to find that a significant number were true of me. It had me wonder how often a more sensitive child is written off in our society, teased, urged towards toughness as I was, when it is simply not their nature. I expect that in this process many natural gifts are undervalued, remain hidden or are lost.

My interior life provided respite and I happily spend time alone, loved to read, and drew on every scrap of paper I could find. Once, when quite young, I completed a colored pencil drawing of cowboys and horses of which I was quite proud, created on a small section of wall in an upstairs hallway. For this I was spanked and badly shamed, a shame that intensified as I watched my mother scrub that wall until the wallpaper shredded and had to be replaced. It did not quite match the rest of the hallway as the existing paper had faded somewhat, and thus became a troubling eyesore for my mother that was commented on for many months to come.

******

I have some sweet memories of St. Matthews church-- the tangible new hope of Easter, the chancel rife with lilies, their perfume drifting through the sanctuary, or midnight services on Christmas Eve in that cold, expectant, and candlelit space normally seen only in daylight. I treasured the sense of family there, the sweet notes of Bach pouring from the organ, the stained-glass window presented by the Ladies Aid Society and purchased with hard earned pennies in the 1930's.

There was, however, much in religion that troubled me, even at a young age. So many lessons seemed contradictory, like pieces of a jigsaw puzzle that stubbornly would not fit. Sunday school teachers repeatedly told us that "God is love" yet the scriptures read at church services spoke of a God whose actions seemed without compassion or love; a God of vindictive anger that one could only fear. The examples were many: God's demand that Abraham slaughter his son Isaac to demonstrate his faithfulness; the story of Job, "a man blameless and upright" who was made to suffer unspeakable loss to prove his devotion; the vengeful assault on Lot's wife, who looked back with sadness at the death of her friends and the destruction of her home and was thus turned into a pillar of salt. How, I wondered, could this be a God whose love we could trust when he seemed so quick to cruelly condemn? And why was I considered sinful; what terrible thing had I done? This Christian concept of original sin -- in Calvinism known as "total hereditary depravity" – is illustrated by a letter from the Youth for Christ radio program, postmarked January 10, 1955 and addressed to nine-year-old me:

Dear Little Listener:

Enclosed is the prize I promised you for guessing the name of the song. This little gift will always remind you of God's greatest gift His Son. Remember that He loves you and thus died. FOR GOD SO LOVED THE WORLD THAT HE GAVE HIS ONLY BEGOTTEN SON THAT WHOSOEVER BELIEVETH ON HIM SHOULD NOT PERISH BUT HAVE EVERLASTING LIFE.

Why did Jesus have to die? Because he wanted to pay for our sins! You see, God the Father made a rule that anyone that committed sin even one sin, would have to pay for it by being punished forever. You might think that this is an awfully hard rule--but remember that God is so good that He can't bear to look upon even one little sin. How would (you) like it if you went to a party and you had on a nice clean white dress or suit and someone put just one tiny black inkspot on it, right in front? It wouldn't feel clean and white to you anymore, would it? You'd want to hurry right back home and put on another clean dress or suit! You see, just one tiny black inkspot spoiled it. And that's the way God would feel about even one little sin -- in fact, much more so--because God is perfect.

And so it would seem to us that nobody would ever have a chance of getting to heaven, because we all know that everyone sins, even little boys and girls. But God knows that, too--and even though we are sinners and really deserve to go to Hell, God still loves us. Not only that, but He can't bear the thought of even one person going to Hell because the Bible says that He is not willing that any should perish. Now just because He loves us and does not want us to go to Hell, does that mean that he will break his own law and let us go to Heaven with all of our sins? Oh, no! God does not lie: If He says that sins have to be paid for--well somebody is going to have to pay for them. God really had a problem, didn't he? How was He going to get us to Heaven and still get our sins paid for? Do you want to know how He solved it? Well, I'll tell you. He said, I passed a law that sins will have to be paid for--so I'll pay for them myself. I will send my only Son, whom I love above everything, to die on the cross for all sinners. And when sin is paid for, I'll raise him from the dead and make another rule so that the men, women, boys and girls who trust in my Son, Jesus Christ, and believe that He died for their sins can be sure of going to Heaven.

And what do you think! Everything happened just exactly as God planned it. Jesus Christ came to earth, lived a life without sin and then, of His own free will, died on the cross to pay for your sins and mine. And now--all you have to do is to believe that Jesus died especially for you and God will see to it that you'll go to Heaven where you'll live happily forever and ever and ever--just like in fairy tales--except that this is TRUE AND REAL!

Will you believe that Jesus died for you? Then write and tell me that you will. And I'll send you a nice new testament and a red pencil to mark the verses that Mr. Benge will tell you about on the radio every day at 10:30 on WBMD. Now the Lord bless you--REAL GOOD! DON'T FORGET TO WRITE!

Sincerely in Christ,

Rita J. Mull, Secretary, Youth for Christ

The adults in my life seemed certain of our sin, convinced that we had entered this world dirty in the eyes of God and in need of atonement, a God that seemed to have set us up just to save us; to my mind an essential betrayal. Yet I was fearful that this merciless God could see my thoughts as our minister assured us that he did. So, I sat quietly in church, attempting to be devout, hoping for something akin to a lightning strike. But if my thoughts were sinful, if this cruel God were real, I worried that I would be condemned to Hell no matter what else might be good about me. As I grew older the biblical stories, easily believed as a small child, became harder to accept. I'd been taught that one does not look for proof but accepts on faith – a faith I struggled to have. I did not express any of this, not wanting to publicize my disbelief, be disgraced nor confirm that I was the outlier that I truly seemed to be.

******

Nature provided the spirituality I did not find in church, and there were two rural places that were a constant pleasure and comfort to me: my Uncle Harry's farm in the Randallstown area outside Baltimore city and my grandmother's dearly loved home on Kent Island.

Several times a year we would travel to Uncle Harry's, sometimes to visit, often to obtain vegetables that my mother would freeze or can. Once, when farm laborers were in short supply, we spent several Saturdays picking apples from ladders high in the trees.

The entrance to the farm was by way of a narrow lane that ran between two stone houses that stood like sentinels facing Old Court Road. The lane veered to the right, its gravel surface dipping into a hollow and then rising slowly towards the farmhouse which was set in a wide green lawn studded with maples and shrubbery. The house was of wood siding and painted bright white. The foundation was of local stone that had a high mica content, and I was intrigued by its shimmering veins of light. After the required greetings, I was free to leave the adults behind and escape outside into this magical world. Past the house were an assortment of outbuildings and dusty lanes leading to the far reaches of the farm. The nearby barns were well kept, painted crisp white with dark green trim. The first was built into a sloping hillside, the interior cool and dark and smelling of earth and old apples. The second housed the dairy herd, its loft packed with fresh hay. An adjoining room held large, lidded bins of grain guarded by a squad of feral cats. Behind the barn the apple orchard

stretched into the distance, the old varietal names like a litany -
Baldwin, Cortland, McIntosh, Northern Spy, Spitzenburg, Winesap.
There were sheds housing wagons, plows and corn shellers and a lane
that passed a pen of noisy pigs and a chicken yard of white leghorns.
At the end of that lane an iron gate opened to the lower pasture
where the Guernsey herd grazed or napped beneath the trees.

There were additional lanes that wound along the edges of
fields that in summer were abundant with corn, tomatoes, squashes,
pumpkins, potatoes and beans. Past the fields and deep into the
farm, the lane forded a stream that ran at the base of a hillside
studded with young trees. Roaming there one early spring, I found
that hillside lush with wild violets, their pansy-shaped faces in shades
of purple, periwinkle, orchid, cream, lemon and lilac. I stood in that
dusty lane, struck into stillness by its beauty, transfixed by a
sacredness I never found in church.

My grandmother's farm on Kent Island was another
sanctuary. The garden and fields, the pine woods and creek offered
an ever-changing seasonal display of nature's bounty in the colors
and patterns of shells, bird feathers, plants, and marsh as well as the
wide expanse of sky, sand, creek and river. This much-loved place
had me feel as though I was nestling into the world as it should be.
The shrubbery garden held hummingbird nests with eggs smaller
than jellybeans, cicada sang in the bleached light of noon, fields
untilled since my grandfather's passing were now rich with blackberry
canes, cornflower, daisies & Queen Anne's Lace. There were cherry,

15

apple and pear trees, willows, black walnut, mulberry and pine; a strawberry patch, a grape arbor, the well's cold water, the antique milk house roofed in moss covered slate. There was the call of the bob white from the farthest field at dusk, quiet nights when the sky blazed with stars, the barn loft where one could feel the past breathing, my great-grandfather's law books, the box of tomahawks and arrowheads turned up by my grandfather's plow.

I would walk the sandy lane to the creek, swatting at gnats, watching the swaying marsh grass and cattails green and golden in summer and the white egret stalking fish in the shallows. The ever-changing tone of the creek varied according to the water's depth, the weather and the season, olive, turquoise, ultramarine, indigo, jade. We fished and crabbed on waters that opened to the Chester River, then to the Chesapeake and on to the Atlantic and worlds far away. The marsh grass dried to ochre and sienna as the seasons shifted. There were ducks in flight against a bright cobalt sky and ice formed at the edges of the marsh. I roamed the woodlot, its floor deep with spent pine needles, dappled golden by sunbeams breaking through the high branches of the Loblolly pines. Here holly, Indian pipes and jack-in-the-pulpit bloomed in the damp. I collected things - wild berries that my grandmother would bake in a dessert, baskets of pinecones to be used as kindling for her woodstove in winter, wildflower bouquets, soft crabs and fish, and once an entire shoebox filled with the fragile shells of the 17-year cicada collected from the bark of the mulberry tree.

My maternal grandmother was born in 1879. She was a woman of kindness and warmth, who had worked hard much of her life and now in her 80's sat on her porch with the peaceful stillness of a Buddha. When I was with her, I never felt judged or pushed into a mold. These two rural places were where I felt most free, most safe, with people who required nothing more of me than being myself, a generosity that my child self could not have named, and my adult self has never forgotten.

When we visited Kent Island, I would often be left behind in the care of my grandmother. On one such visit we were having lunch on the porch before my parents and brother would begin their drive back to Baltimore. Gary, my frequent tormentor, was four years older and considerably larger, so our encounters did not go well for me. On this occasion he kicked me sharply under the table.

"Stop it! I squealed.

He raised his hands in mock innocence, took another bite of his sandwich and kicked me again.

I cried out again, sure that our mother, the usual disciplinarian, would intervene but there was no reaction. Gary smirked at me across the table and landed another kick to my shin.

I bounced out of my chair, shouting "Leave me alone!"

My mother exploded. Not at him, but at me. I had disrupted lunch.

I pushed my chair back so hard that it tumbled, and I bolted from the porch, letting the screen door slam hard behind me. I ran to the woods, climbed a tree and sat in the crook of a branch fighting back tears. It seemed to me that in my mother's eyes, my brother could do no wrong, and my tears were ones of anger over her unfairness, but more so over my powerlessness which seemed so absolute. I stayed in that tree for what seemed a very long time. Eventually, Gary came and stood at its base.

"I've been looking all over for you!' he said. "We're getting ready to leave and Mom said you should come and say goodbye."

I glared down at him. "I hate you" I said with all the venom I could rally. "Go away."

And he did.

No one else came in search of me and I stubbornly stayed in that tree, feeling that to return was to capitulate, to agree to a compromise I would not make; a tiny piece of power claimed. And at that moment, torn between love and hate, I didn't want to see my mother. It was only after our Chevy disappeared down the sandy lane that I climbed down, crossing the sunny lawn to the porch. When I entered, my grandmother put out her arms to me. Wrapped in her hug, she whispered in my ear. "Your mother was wrong. I make it my business not to interfere with my children, but your mother was wrong. And I told her so."

God, how I loved that woman. She could see me. Years later I discovered the work of Welsh poet Dylan Thomas. His poem "Fern Hill" encapsulated the joy and freedom I felt in both of those dearly loved places of my childhood as well as my now adult knowledge that nothing, not even that which we deeply love, can be kept.

******

My elementary school was comprised of two buildings of dark brick, known to us as the "new" and the "old" buildings, though in truth both buildings were long outdated. My paternal grandmother's younger brother Melvin, born in 1897, attended school here, as had my father, born in 1912. While there were inadequacies that this worn school displayed - desk tops lumpy with the carvings of predecessors, lavatories with missing stall doors, lunch served on dented compartmentalized metal trays worthy of a prison, there was still much in these old buildings my eye appreciated - big windows and sunlit rooms, wide stairwells, Victorian cloakrooms with rows of iron coat hooks, wooden flooring worn to a burnished golden brown by many feet and moppings.

High ceilinged classrooms opened off a central hallway on each floor, their banks of windows covered in yellowed paper shades through which the afternoon sun gave a soft golden glow. Over the years I was assigned to different classroom locations and to a variety of teachers, some kind, others cold, none more memorable than Miss Kathleen Moore who each afternoon would have us push our desks against the wall in order to make room for dancing. She taught us the waltz, tango and rhumba, giving out strips of colored ribbon as prizes for successfully mastering the steps. Surprisingly, I was good at this, and along with Sonny Marek became the star dancing duo. Around this time, I also started to attend the periodic sixth grade dances held in the gym where I was never without a partner. This brought a surprising change, a brief elevation in my standing with my peers and with it an enjoyable sense of inclusion. It was an unexpected rise from obscurity that, unfortunately, wasn't to last.

I don't remember what errand took me past Mrs. Jaworski's music room one December afternoon. It was a room I knew well, a place where we sang Appalachian folksongs and Depression era ditties while Mrs. Jaworski banged out the tunes on her piano. It was here that we cringed at the recording of Boris Karloff and the Vienna State Opera Orchestra's rendition of Prokofiev's "Peter and the Wolf" which we heard with great regularity when Mrs. Jaworski was not in a piano-playing mood. On this afternoon, a student choir was practicing for an upcoming Christmas concert. The yellowed window shades gave the room its usual golden glow and chalk dust floated in the errant beams as the choir launched into a melancholy tune I'd not heard before.

Toyland, toy land

Li-ittle girl and boy land

While you dwell within it

You are ever happy there

Childhood's joy land

Mi-istic merry toy land

Once you pass its borders

You can ne'er return again

I knew in an instant, struck still in that hallway that smelled of stale lunches and orange peel, that I was there, hovering at the edge of my childhood, the future provocative and unknown. The signs had been there, unacknowledged and misunderstood, most certainly around Christmas which had lost its magic, and where toys had been replaced with socks. The world shifted that afternoon in the golden hallway outside of Mrs. Jaworski's music room. I felt as though I hung by my toes at the edges of that song in a mosaic of feelings - anticipation of new adventures, a sense of excitement with equal dollops of apprehension and sadness at leaving something known behind.

*****

Somewhere around age ten, the pattern of my home life changed to include housework. I was first taught to iron, starting with the handkerchiefs my father wore in his jacket pocket each day and working up to larger and more complicated pieces. I helped with dinner preparation and afterwards dried the dishes and helped clean

21

up the kitchen before beginning my homework. At some point my mother took on the job of cleaning the church each Saturday and I was drafted to help. The job paid five dollars and I was given a dollar for completing my assigned tasks - picking up abandoned bulletins and newsletters from the previous week, righting the bibles and hymnals in their racks, dusting the pews, pulpits and altar and running the vacuum on the red carpet of the aisle and chancel. Saturdays were outdoor cleaning day as well. The rowhouses of our neighborhood were of brick, two storied with basement. All had covered porches trimmed in heavy slabs of marble and this marble as well as the linoleum covered flooring needed to be scrubbed. Once a week. In all weather. By me. My porch-cleaning services were also volunteered to several widows in the neighborhood, but when one woman gave me a quarter tip, my mother made me return the coin. It was, she said, my Christian duty to help others. I also became the errand runner of choice, picking up needed items from our neighborhood grocery store, carrying my father's suits to the drycleaners, toting shoes to the cobbler for new soles or heels. My brother's chores seemed relatively few. Under duress, he cut our tiny plot of grass in season and when a winter storm hit, he shoveled snow from our front walk. How odd that this distribution of work seems so lopsided to me now, though it seemed normal and acceptable at the time. It is, I think, a demonstration of the fish-to-water analogy, the fact that what surrounds you becomes normal, invisible or unseen because it is all that you know. In the 1950's such gender inequality was not questioned and training young women for domestic duty rather than a career was often a given. It never occurred to me to question it or to protest. A fish can't distinguish water until they aren't in it; I couldn't see the limits of my world until I stepped outside.

2 Adolescence

The world which had provided some semblance of belonging in my younger years changed significantly between sixth grade and high school. It was as though a switch had been flipped, so that without comprehending how or why, I had slipped from being somewhat acceptable to simply not being good enough. It was a judgment demonstrated by the teasing of my peers at both church and school. I found myself dismissed, rejected, and it seeped into me like an infection. What had changed? I felt myself to be the same person inside, but my outside had altered, grown plump in the hormonal flood of adolescence. I discovered that our church, a niche I had trusted to be a place of love and safety, could be as mean as any in the outside world. One boy – Billy Reynolds -- taunted me mercilessly. At first, I was simply astonished. As it continued, I became overwhelmed and wondered how it was possible that no one heard his taunts and if they did, why no one intervened. I finally admitted my misery to my mother, hoping that she would mention my suffering to his mother and thus put an end to the abuse. My mother, who had often declared me to be "too sensitive" and in need of "toughing up", gave advice that did not ease my discomfort. "You have to stand up for yourself" she said. With an eye-for-an-eye approach, she advised that I begin to call my attacker "pimple face" as he had an unruly case of acne.

"Stand up for yourself" sounds easy except when you do not feel strong enough to do so. I was not brave enough for confrontation and felt it would only bring further grief. To my mind, her response did not touch the core of what had gone so bad for me. What I wanted was protection. So, I remained quiet, sitting in Sunday night youth group, perpetually feigning cold and wearing my coat, trying to hide the body that inspired ridicule.

That summer our young minister decided that the youth group should produce a play and I was given a prime part. Yearning for acceptance, I memorized the script carefully, seeing this as an opportunity to prove myself worthy, to be acceptable, perhaps even to shine. On opening night, the cast was to enter the stage in darkness and take our positions. I was to be seated on a low stool, a spot I had occupied through many rehearsals. When I sat down that evening, the stool loudly collapsed, banging my head against the wall and leaving me sprawled on the floor. At first I was stunned, then my mind quickly excused it as an accident, but as I lay there in the dark before the lights were turned up, the truth sunk in: the collapse had been instantaneous; the stool had been tampered with. And the message was clear: the fat girl broke the stool. The audience knew nothing of this, of course, and I went on with my part as if nothing had happened, though I wished many times afterward that I'd been quick thinking or brave enough to find my way to the door and disappear into the night. There were other incidents, but this one crushed me in a way that no others had. This one place where I had felt safe no longer was; the Christian lessons of love were empty words. Feeling powerless to change my circumstances I continued onward, attempting to protect myself by pretending not to care, starting out to school and church as required, functioning as unobtrusively as possible, smiling as a deflective mechanism, and pretending to ignore the barbs, while hoping that a new lipstick or blouse, a memorized bible verse or well written paper would somehow save me. I was embarrassed to be.

******

If you've seen the movie Hairspray, especially the musical remake, you've seen a wonderfully sanitized version of the 1960's East Baltimore where I grew up. In truth, Highlandtown and Patterson High School were additional pieces of my adolescent hell. While my figure in 1963 never approached the plumpness of Water's Tracy Turnblad, my body continued to be a focus of derision. And although Tracy seemed blissfully untroubled by her waistline, and while other characters in the film took no issue with her thickset body, in the real world even slightly chubby girls often face daily rejection.

While overt meanness was rare at Patterson, those of us who did not measure up were unwelcome rejects in our homeroom class of slim and stylish "sorority" girls. We were too plump, too skinny, not pretty enough. We came from different backgrounds or didn't dress stylishly -- some due to affordability -- me because even in 1963, my mother was still living in the throes of the Great Depression and sewing my ill-fitting clothes or buying them second hand.

East Baltimore was blue-collar. My father and the fathers of most everyone I knew worked in Baltimore's factories - Bethlehem Steel, Domino Sugar, Crosse and Blackwell, McCormick Spices, Western Electric, Lever Brothers - although many of my schoolmates, as well as cousins in other branches of our family, did not seem to operate under the same austerity as I. I was envious of their outfits purchased at department stores; they had charm bracelets, hair curlers, the most recent record releases, movie magazines and purses to hold their dollar bills. Of course, there were girls at school from families poorer than mine, girls with gray skin and unkempt hair and clothing, who hid their gaze as often as I did mine.

In our homeroom class we were seated in strict alphabetical order, where my spectacular good luck placed me at the back of the room with Kathy and Olga, two of the more venomous girls in our class. They wore impossibly short skirts, giggled together over their sexual experiences and delighted in inquiring of mine, knowing full well that girls like myself would have none to share. They sniggered at my ignorance and virginity. I was enrolled as a Business Education major at the insistence of my mother, who pushed me towards the secretarial career she had once longed for. The subjects I enjoyed -

history, art and writing - had long ago been judged frivolous and impractical, with no possibility for earning a paycheck.

"Taking the academic course would be of no use to you anyway" my mother reasoned. "There is no money for you to go to college but if you take the business classes you can always find a job."

I asked why there was no money for me. There had, after all, been money for tuition plus room and board for Gary's education at an out-of-state college.

"That's different" my mother said. "Boys need an education". She further buttressed her position by stating that I was not equipped for academic work, a recitation of her long-held opinion that I was "not good at math", a result of my never buckling down to those multiplication tables at age seven. I expect she reasoned that I could have some measure of financial security in adulthood with the office career she championed. I can imagine her thinking "my daughter is overweight, not exceptionally pretty and a bit dreamy-headed. Who knows if she will ever find a husband? At least if she can type............".

There were two bright spots in my high school experience: Miss Poteet's art class and a journalism class taught by Miss Carolyn Baldwin. Miss Baldwin also oversaw the production of the school's weekly newspaper and appointed me as one of five student editors, a position I greatly enjoyed, and which gave my self-esteem a boost. The students I interacted with in the press room were mostly academic course majors with plans for continuing their education. It seemed that they had far brighter futures than I and I wished, not for the first time, that my parents had allowed me a wider education. As graduation approached, my future loomed as a dark dead end. With no academic background nor the funding needed for additional schooling, I felt that I was without options. Typing, shorthand and bookkeeping left me feeling numb, soulless and palsied. I hated all the prim little snots with steno pads that were so sure of their way in the world. I slogged through shorthand classes, only at the last-minute building enough speed to qualify for graduation. It was like trudging through mud. At times it seemed as though I were holding my breath, waiting for real life to begin. I longed for something else, whatever else but this; wanting more, knowing that there must be more, wanting something that which I could not even articulate.

There were no school buses in 1963 and we rode the public buses of the Baltimore Transit Company. Painted bright acid yellow, green and white they had worn suspensions and cracked leather seats of dull brown or muddy olive green. To travel to and from school I rode two bus lines, transferring near the commercial center of Highlandtown. In these days before malls, this Eastern Avenue shopping area contained several blocks of department stores, small retail shops and restaurants. Alone after school, I would roam down the avenue, studying the beautiful clothing in the wide display windows of the Princess Shops, Irvin's, and Epstein's. At the turquoise storefront of Stella's Bridal Shop, I coveted the frothy multi-colored prom dresses and fantasized a world of acceptance and boyfriends.

Those afternoons on the "Avenue" were also demonstrations of my two discordant and irreconcilable desires. While the shop windows displayed the tiny stylish outfits I longed to wear, here also were a nearly endless variety of enticing foods, tempting my always present and driving physical hunger. Woolworth's five-and-dime held out the possibility of teenage normalcy with its displays of Tangee lipsticks, powder compacts, manicure kits and pink diaries with heart-shaped locks. But they also had a cart selling submarine sandwiches and a lunch counter hung with posters of cheeseburgers and hot fudge sundaes. Confectionary store shelves were heaped with 5-cent candy bars, bags of pretzels and potato chips and trays of candied and caramel dipped apples. The G & A diner specialized in hotdogs and had a large grill in the front window tempting passersby with the aroma of hot sausages, plump fresh rolls, onions and spiced chili sauce. On the southwest corner of Bank and Conkling streets was Hoehn's, the sort of bakery that could once be found on nearly every Baltimore corner, the sweet smell of yeast, sugar and hot fat dissolving my resolve, pulling me off the sidewalk to behold the polished glass cases filled with honey dips, crullers, éclairs, and custard filled fantasies sprinkled with confectioner's sugar. At 4:00 in the afternoon, with lunch long past and dinner in the distant future, I struggled mightily against hunger and temptation though, here too, I lost more battles than I won.

There was a dearth of dietary advice and support in the 1960's. Magazines cheerily advised that one should "just eat less" as though that thought had not occurred to their readers. For the desperate there were vile tasting AYDS chewable "candies" which were purported to blunt hunger. I begged for money to buy them, naively believing the ads that promised effortless success. When no financial assistance was forthcoming, I hoarded all the coins that came my way and stole money from my mother's purse to buy them. Other equally expensive options included Metrecal liquid which was taken in lieu of meals, and before the advent of diet soda, expensive ill-tasting sugar-free drinks manufactured for diabetics. Magazine and newspaper advertisements promoted expensive machines such as the belted "jiggler" guaranteed to shake your body to a slender ideal, roller machines that promised to pound fleshy thighs to slimness and sauna suits that promised an unrealistic weight loss of five pounds per day. Jack LaLanne was available on our black and white TV on weekday mornings when school wasn't in session.

My dad's sister, my sweet aunt Mildred, had struggled with her weight her entire life so she likely sympathized but had no solution to offer. Once she took me shopping for an Easter outfit at the Lane Bryant store downtown. For years thereafter the Lane Bryant Company sent me their monthly newsletter entitled "Chubby Club News". Gary, anticipating the arrival of Mad magazine or secret decoder rings, often pounced upon the mail. The arrival of the "Chubby Club News" sent him shrieking through the house announcing its arrival. He laughed; my mother laughed. I raged. I still wonder what sort of astonishingly insensitive adult titled that hated piece of mail.

When I looked at the beautiful prom gowns in the window of Stella's Bridal Shop, I wished for a Prince Charming, but I longed more fervently for a savior, someone to rescue me from the dreaded approaching doom of an office job where I would type memos, answer phones and struggle with shorthand and my dress size for the rest of my life.

******

Saviors come in unpredictable forms.

One morning as I sat enduring the torments of Olga and Kathy, a voice came over the sound system requesting my presence in the counselor's office. A summons from the office was most often of a disciplinary nature, and a hoot went up from the class with several people wondering aloud as to what I had done. I scurried down the vacant hallways to Dr. Thompson's office, my mind racing. This was so unusual that I quickly assumed the worst. Maybe I wasn't going to graduate. Was my shorthand speed too low? Would I have to repeat the year or go to summer school? What would my mother say?

Dr. Thompson looked up as I was ushered into her office, giving me a thin smile and producing a manila folder from the papers on her desk. I stood rigidly before her desk waiting for the ax to fall.

"Miss Poteet tells me that you are the best student in her art class. Do you like art?"

"Oh, yes M'am" I said with relief. "Very much."

"Do you want to continue with more education?"

"Yes, M'am. I'd like to but......"

"Excellent. A vast improvement over the goals of most of your classmates."

She turned her attention to the manila folder, extracting several sheets of paper.

"Each year, every Baltimore high school receives a one-year scholarship to the Maryland Institute College of Art to be given to a deserving student. Do you know the school?"

I didn't know it. I sensed a thread of salvation here but feared it might ebb in the face of my ignorance.

"No ma'am" I answered.

"Well, it is a rather well known. I'm authorized to give the scholarship to a qualified student. Do you want it?"

Did I want it? I did, oh, I did.

She told me that I would be required to submit examples of my artwork to the school for approval and indicated the number I should call to set up an appointment.

"And you will have to get your parents approval, of course" she added. "There is a space for them to sign at the bottom."

Parental approval? In my joy, I hadn't considered that. But I felt I had just been thrown a lifeline and I was determined to not let go. I fairly danced through the remaining school day, composing in my mind a winning conversation with my parents.

"Absolutely not" said my mother. "You've taken secretarial courses so you could get a good job."

"But I don't want those jobs!" I said. "And it is a really good school. It is accredited, and it's right here in town."

"Completely out of the question" she answered. "Besides, we can't afford it."

"There is nothing to afford! The scholarship covers tuition and fees for the year. I could get a part time job to pay for my supplies."

"We'd still be putting a roof over your head."

Ah, the roof. Never had my value been made so clear.

Over the weekend, I tried repeatedly and unsuccessfully to make my case. More objections to the scholarship surfaced. She disapproved of the school. It was a wicked place, full of hippies. No place for a nice girl.

"Did you know that they have nude models?" she asked. "I've heard that students have to undress and take turns modeling in class. How do you feel about that?"

I didn't believe her. I continued my attempts to convince her, but she was unmoved. Whether by genetics or training, I had always been the dutiful, follow-the-rules, docile child, but now I was angry, resentful of her hard position and unwillingness to be supportive of this opportunity I wanted so badly. I hated the fact that I had no power or money and that made my needs and wishes subordinate to her seemingly irrational views. But wanting the scholarship made me brave and argumentative in a way I'd never been before; it was as if I had discovered a new level of strength, a solidity at my core that I'd not experienced before, a flicker of the independence that would one day have me leave my parent's home and step out into a different world.

"Oh, let her do it" I heard my father say after I once again retreated angrily to my room. "It is only for a year. She'll get it out of her system. What would be the harm?"

That was the only conversation I overheard, although I am certain there were many more, my sweet father lobbying on my behalf before my mother at last relented. I've always known I had him to thank for my reprieve.

3 Maryland Institute College of Art

The Maryland Institute College of Art's (MICA) beautiful 1905 Renaissance Revival building is four stories high and stands on a hill north of downtown Baltimore. Nothing in the architecture of East Baltimore prepared me for it. The exterior is of marble, hewn from the same local quarries that supplied marble for the U.S. Capital and the Washington monument. An exterior marble staircase led to ornate bronze doors that opened into an elegant, vaulted entry. I stepped from the bright sunlight of an August afternoon into a quiet, cool space softly lit by skylights. Additional stairs led to an interior courtyard modeled after an Italian villa. The floors were of intricate mosaic design and an arched colonnade spanned three sides of the courtyard, supported by columns of red marble with a decorative frieze bearing the names of art legends: Bernini, Ghiberti, Cellini, Palladio, Giotto, Raphael, Michelangelo Buonarroti. Reproductions of classical statues stood at the base of an elegant split staircase which curved towards the next floor, its ornate brass railing softly gleaming in the diffused light. What a wondrous place I had landed! Around the perimeter of the courtyard were doors opening to offices, a small library and classrooms. The distant clack of a typewriter led me to a reception area where a secretary directed me to the faculty member who approved my portfolio. I was given a copy of the freshman foundation curriculum, a schedule of classes, a reading list for the required academic courses, and a directory of local art supply and bookstores where these needed items could be found.

With Dr. Thompson's help I found a summer job at the Beneficial Finance Company on Eastern Avenue where I answered phones, typed letters and tracked on little yellow cards the outrageous interest payments charged their borrowers. I saved nearly every penny of my salary. I pored over the college issue of "Seventeen" magazine, the consummate authority on what the well-dressed college freshman should wear. I purchased a navy A-line skirt with a fake alligator belt, a blouse, and several sweaters, saving most of my dollars for books and supplies.

When I entered MICA in September the entire student body had returned, most clad in paint-stained jeans, tee shirts and tie-dye. Nearly everyone smoked cigarettes; some students brought their dogs to roam the building. One enterprising young woman sold jewelry purchased in the hipper world of Greenwich Village from a booth in the school café. There was a wondrous air of freedom about the place. Everyone was cool. Genial. People talked to me. I had somehow left behind the previously inescapable slot I had occupied in my East

Baltimore world. The tailored blouse and A-line skirt were, of course, completely out of place and impractical as well. To my mother's growing distress, I soon began wearing jeans and tees more appropriate to the studio. I took up smoking though never brave enough to do so in my parent's presence. Working on assignments in my room late at night, I would sometimes smoke, hiding my ashtray of cold butts in the drawer of my nightstand. Apparently, my secret was not well kept, as often my mother would empty and wash it, taping to it newspaper clippings about lung cancer. What else, I thought, was she doing in my room? I could imagine her going through my bureau drawers, reading my notebooks. There was no privacy here.

Two of my new school friends offered to pierce my ears. I wanted to do it, seduced by the beautiful Greenwich Village earrings for sale in the cafe. I knew my mother would disapprove thus I fully expected to be chastised for my choice when I returned home that afternoon. As expected, she railed against the "heathenish practice" of ear piercing, suggesting that I move to Africa where I could now fit in with the natives.

"Why didn't you get one in your nose, too?" she asked.

"My ears are pierced" said a firm voice from the rocking chair by the window. It was her mother, my adored grandmother, who was visiting from Kent Island. She went on to say that pierced ears had been very fashionable at the turn of the century when she was young and wasn't it nice that they were coming back in style. My mother stopped her tirade. I thanked my grandmother with a silent smile. Did I say how much I loved that woman?

******

School was a joyful and exciting discovery of new subjects, new ideas, and new ways of thinking. I was determined to learn from all that was put before me, though some courses were a struggle. My secretarial training left me ill-prepared for courses such as the geometry-based Systems of Projection, and I quickly realized that my exposure to literature, world history, geography, languages and creative writing had been meager or non-existent. The religious indoctrination of my youth was solidly jarred by some of the subject matter, including the history professor who asserted from his podium that Saint Paul had been the worst thing that ever happened to Christianity. I discovered that my art experience and views were limited as well. Paints had been in short supply in our high school art classes and we had worked in watercolor washes on paper or with poster paint on rigid canvas boards. MICA's foundation painting classes introduced me to the beauty of oil paints. I loved their rich color, lushness and luminosity and wanted every shade displayed at the art supply store -- lemon, chrome and indian yellows; olive, sap, emerald and viridian greens; cadmium orange and red; violet, carmine, alizarin crimson, rose doré; Prussian, ultramarine, pthalo, cobalt, cerulean and turquoise blues; rich earth tones of ochre, burnt and raw siennas and umbers. I abandoned the unbending canvas boards and learned to stretch canvases, priming them as instructed with rabbit skin glue followed by a coat of lead-based paint. My previous instructors had revered realism as the only true art, but now I dove into the works of Degas, Cezanne, Toulouse-Lautrec, Van Gogh, Picasso, Braque, and Matisse, their paintings cascading into my consciousness in a bounty of shape, texture and color.

Only two years before my arrival at MICA, Eugene "Bud" Leake, a graduate of Yale's School of Art and Architecture had arrived to take on its presidency. He had a large vision for the institution, including an expansion of the fine arts department. He upgraded the faculty by hiring a number of gifted artists for teaching positions at the school. Glenn McNatt reported in the Baltimore Sun that Leake took on "the task of reviving the nearly moribund Maryland Institute" and "recruited the best artists he could find as teachers, among them the painters Grace Hartigan and Raoul Middleman, sculptors Norman Carlberg and Stephanie Scuris and painter-printmaker Peter Milton."[i]

Abby Sangiamo's basic drawing class provided a series of ever changing and interesting assignments. The entertaining Raoul Middleman taught painting as well as an introductory course in color that included intriguing and difficult assignments executed from the 220 color variations found in the paper options of a Color-aid pack. Peter Milton, a recent Yale MFA grad and future master printmaker, taught Basic Design where we worked in assigned teams on large projects assembled from various print styles. I was immersed in lectures, readings and class assignments, and, excited by all the new information and the possibilities I could not have imagined in high school.

The neighborhood surrounding the school was also far different from the streets I knew in East Baltimore. I had been ignorant of much of Baltimore's history, so the nearby streets offered yet another window for learning. MICA had no dorms in the 1960's, so out of town students found apartments in the surrounding community of Bolton Hill, an historic neighborhood of late 19th century town homes now on the National Register of Historic Places. Bolton Hill had once been a significant address, but over the years it had declined, with many of the classic homes having been cut into low income apartments during World War II. The area was now undergoing a Renaissance, with many of its three and four-storied homes being reclaimed and restored. Most of these homes were of brick or stone and were graced with fine woodwork, stained glass, balconies, attached carriage houses, and large back gardens. The streets were tree-lined, and the neighborhood was scattered with small parks, fountains, statuary, monuments, and flower beds. I learned that these houses were once home to college presidents and deans, wealthy businessmen and merchants, lawyers, architects, artists and authors including F. Scott Fitzgerald, Edith Hamilton, Gertrude Stein, Russell Baker, Sidney Lanier, future U.S. President Woodrow Wilson, and many of the leading physicians and scientists at Johns Hopkins University.

The people I met at MICA were also outside my East Baltimore experience, and came from many different backgrounds and exposures. I met Singy Tevis in Milton's basic design class and we became lifelong friends. A day student like me, she drove in each day from the town of Westminster. Her family was wealthy and far more sophisticated than my own, but one of the delights of MICA was that class and money rarely mattered. Singy could be audacious, intrepidly daring and bold; in essence the very opposite of me. She was tiny, a small and wiry size two with strongly held opinions and a high level of energy. While the world had always occurred for me as a place requiring great caution, for Singy it was a playground. While I had learned to be guarded and play it safe, Singy often made choices with no expectation of negative outcomes. I saw through her that spontaneity and fun were often missing in my life. Singy was good for me because she would not accept my cautious hesitations but pushed me to try new things and take more risks.

The politics of my new classmates was far more liberal than the conservative stance I'd grown up with, and the 1960's were, of course, a time of ferment and change. The outside world suddenly felt agitated and unsettled. The previous year had been dominated by the Cuban Missile Crisis and the expansion of the civil rights movement, including federal intervention and subsequent violence surrounding the admission of James Meredith to the University of Mississippi. Through April and May of 1963, the Southern Christian Leadership Conference designed a series of peaceful demonstrations that resulted in attacks by the police and the arrest of Dr. Martin Luther King. In June, President Kennedy federalized Alabama's National Guard in order to facilitate the entrance of black students at the University of Alabama and introduced Civil Rights legislation to Congress. Also in June, NAACP field officer Medgar Evers was assassinated in the driveway of his home in Jackson, Mississippi and in August, Dr. Martin Luther King gave his stirring "I Have A Dream" speech at the March on Washington. On September 15, a bomb explosion at the 16th

Street Baptist Church in Birmingham killed four young girls and injured 20 others. My stomach churned at the violence. November 22, 1963 brought a fresh horror. We were working on a joint project in class when Singy's portable radio brought a fevered announcement that President Kennedy had been shot while riding in a motorcade in Dallas. We searched for more information, moving the dial to additional stations but learned nothing more. Our frustration dissolved into confusion; it was frightening and inconceivable that the President could be shot on the streets of America. I left class and caught a bus for home, certain that the television would provide updates on the President's condition. The trip felt surreal. I sat in a window seat listening to the everyday chatter of other passengers who clearly had not heard the news. As our bus lumbered past Baltimore's Civic Center, two uniformed workmen were slowly lowering the American flag and I knew that our President was dead.

******

Given the awakening that the scholarship afforded me, I became determined to stay in school. Since the initial award was for just one year, I began applying for other sources of funding. Ultimately, I cobbled together a Congressional scholarship, a Baltimore City Council scholarship and a MICA work scholarship for which I ran the school's switchboard during the operator's lunch break and typed catalog cards in the library. I entered my sophomore year with full tuition funding and the earnings from that summer's job in the bank. Classes continued to be stimulating and demanding, and I was as joyfully engaged and focused as I had been in my freshman year.

And then I fell in love - crazily, first-time, addictively in love. The girl that boys never seemed to notice was suddenly courted by a handsome 6'4" guy with a great smile who smelled of English Leather cologne. Our instant chemistry stunned me. We had met briefly in a group of friends in the school courtyard, and later at a party where we talked all evening. We were soon inseparable. I was drunk with romance. Immersed. Smitten. Mindless. We could not get enough of each other. As our relationship continued, I also saw signs of trouble that I chose to ignore. Despite Marty's expressed passion for art, he often seemed carelessly indifferent to completing the work that was required. We were not in many of the same classes, but he often mentioned submitting a project late or admitted that he hadn't studied for a test. His roommates would often show up at our early morning history lecture, shrugging their shoulders and reporting that they couldn't get him out of bed. One afternoon Marty told me that he had a paper due the next day but hadn't begun the research. In that moment I was acutely aware of a deep sadness in him; he seemed completely disheartened, so ready to abandon the project, so completely resigned to failure. I couldn't understand how he could just let the assignment go, how he could not at least try. I dragged him to the library in search of reference material, and we worked through the night, putting together an adequate paper with me doing too much of the work. My feelings were scrambled. I felt sympathy for his very real sadness and wondered what had happened that left him without the resolve to do this for himself. I was also annoyed that he had so easily abdicated his responsibility and unsettled by his seemingly indifference regarding his grades. I couldn't fathom how anyone could so easily give up their chance at education, an opportunity I wanted so badly.

Modern discussions addressing student failure list many factors including poor family relationships, previous failures, personality issues, depression, lack of support, poor study habits, lack of motivation, and simply not being ready for the challenges of school and life. I knew that Marty had an unhappy relationship with his family. His father was a corporate executive, his mother a former John Robert Powers model who struggled with mid-life weight gain and was often tipsy before dinner. Their home was lovely, a five-bedroom split-level suburban home at the edge of a golf course. While his parents were very aloof with me, I had grown quite close to Marty's maternal grandmother who made her home with them. She expressed her delight over our relationship, confiding that she had always felt protective of Marty because he was the middle child who often felt passed over or undervalued.

Psychiatrist Alfred Adler (1870-1937) was the first to hypothesize that birth order had a strong effect on a child's character and personality, often affecting their performance and relationships throughout their lives. "Middle child syndrome" as it is called today often results in a strong sense of insecurity, feelings of having been squeezed out or ignored, and can result in a lack of drive and a hopeless life view. While Marty expressed sadness at being a disappointment to his parents, he also expressed a good deal of anger towards them. He was bitter that they seemed to ignore him, focusing their attentions on the academic and sports achievements of his older brother and the adorableness of his younger sister. These many years later, I can see how closely middle child syndrome maps onto Marty's life, but at the time I had no insight at all into his behavior. Wanting him to succeed, I struggled to cover too many bases, trying to complete my own schoolwork and pushing him to do his. I ignored my growing discomfort, refusing to look closely at either the evidence or my increasing distress. I am, at core, an optimistic person, and in this case, I resolutely clung to my rose-colored glasses, just wanting everything to work out. It did not.

Over the summer Marty received a letter from the Provost's office. It referenced an earlier letter in which he had been given a deadline for making up six incomplete credits from his freshman year. It further informed him that since he had not complied with that instruction, he would not be allowed to register for the upcoming term. I was stunned. In all our conversations about school, he had never once mentioned that previous letter. Had he not taken it seriously? Had some sort of magical thinking allowed him to suppose he would escape repercussion? I thought back over the past year, the skipped lectures, the late papers. How, I wondered, had he fared in elementary and high school -- had earlier disappointments developed into defeatism and resignation? And now he was angry. He felt persecuted, though I could not see how he could legitimately feel that way. It troubled me that he seemed to take no responsibility for this failure, but I also felt compassion for his misery. He seemed bleakly defeated, sinking to a dark space I'd not seen before. I was heartsick myself.

We'd been lamenting his having to return home for the summer, but now it seemed he would be returning to Pennsylvania indefinitely.

By the next day Marty seemed somewhat recovered. We sat in the school cafe, and over bitter paper-cup coffee, he laid out a plan.

"We don't need school" he said. "We can have a good life without it. You haven't found funding for next year, so you will probably have to drop out anyway. And now that I've been kicked out, we need a game plan for our future."

He reached across the table and took my hand.

"I love you" he said. "You're the only person I want to be with. We talk all the time about how miserable we are at home, how we want our freedom, and I thought what if we both got jobs? We could save money. We could get married. And we could still go to school; lots of people earn their degrees part time."

Leave school? It hurt my heart to give this up. But Marty was right that I had no money for next fall's tuition. I'd exhausted my scholarship funding and hadn't been focused on locating new sources. And as much as I loved school, I loved him more. I agreed. Ours was the kind of romance found at the cusp of adulthood, when you still have an innocence that tells you that all will turn out well, that there will be a happily-ever-after if you love enough and believe enough in a future that you have no idea how to accomplish, when you have no idea how you will pay the rent or buy groceries, just a blind faith that love will win and all will turn out because you watched all those post World War Two movie reruns on television in the middle of the night.

I found an office job at IBM, bringing my mother's secretarial dream at last to fruition. Marty began work at the Bon Ton department store in York. We enrolled in part time classes at MICA, for which he drove down each Monday and many Saturdays, when we also partied with old friends. I rented an inexpensive hideaway apartment on Charles Street, though we continued to live with our parents, a situation that both of us continued to find oppressive. Marty's parents were embittered over his expulsion from school and now protested his working a "dead end job". My mother, on the other hand, was delighted that I had given up my foolish dream of art school for a "real job", though she objected strongly to my romance with "that boy" who "would never make anything of himself". Goodness knows what she would have said if she had known about that apartment!

In addition to salary, Marty received a substantial store discount, and on Christmas Day he arrived at my parent's home carrying a stack of large and beautifully wrapped gift boxes. They contained clothing from Bon Ton's junior department, lovely outfits, many perfect for my new office career, and all several sizes too small. The cringe worthy message that I needed to lose weight had returned to haunt me. Most women know that clothes that look fantastic on a mannequin often do not translate well to all human bodies. I had a small waist, curvy hips and wore a junior size eleven but these outfits were all size seven and designed for a thinner more angular body. Marty said I would be so beautiful in them and asked me to commit to losing the weight to wear them. Given my body structure it seemed an impossible task. Why was this now of importance?

As time went on our relationship seemed more fragile, though I could not point to a specific reason why. In April Marty ended our relationship. He said many things that didn't make sense, including that I'd never know how much he loved me. We met in the school cafe where I handed back his ring. I had given up so much for him: school, money, virginity (well, in those days that was a serious thing). I was devastated. I had been his champion, but he could not be mine. I couldn't understand why the sun was shining. I cried in my room. My mother said he wasn't worth it. I dragged myself to class.

As the next weekend approached, Singy asked if I was going to attend our group's usual Saturday night get-together at Dave, Nick and Gary's place in the Marlborough Apartments. I said that I didn't feel like going to a party, but Singy, as usual, was unrelenting.

"What are you going to do?" she asked. "Mope around at home listening to your mother say, 'I told you so'? It will be good for you to get out."

I finally agreed, and she was right, it was nice to see everyone. As the evening progressed, I was in the kitchen helping Nick set out refreshments when the front door opened and Marty entered, holding the hand of a tall, slim girl. My friends quickly moved in unison to the foyer, but I stayed out of sight in the kitchen, wishing to avoid a painful meeting, pressing myself against a far wall as though it were a place to hide. I could hear voices but could not distinguish the words. Then the front door slammed, and my friends all returned to the kitchen.

"He said she was just a friend of his" said Nick.

"He didn't think you'd be here" said Gary.

"I said, where the hell did he think you'd be?" said Singy.

"I said he should go back to York" said Dave.

To my knowledge that was the last time any of us heard from him.

Yes, I was devastated by the end of a relationship that had meant so much to me and a future I'd believed in. But my mind used the event to busily dredge up all my old doubts about my self-worth, showing them to me like worn home movies, pointing out that underneath my current discomfort was the clear confirmation that my childhood experiences were true and that so many had been correct about me all along. I just wasn't enough – not loveable enough, interesting enough, strong enough, smart enough, slim enough, pretty enough.

As time went by, I grew angry with myself. Why had I left school and the education I had fought so hard for? Why hadn't I focused on finding new sources of financial aid instead of spending my time helping Marty complete his assignments? Why had I so easily acquiesced to his plan for our future? I now cursed him for his weakness and myself for my blindness. But why all this a surprise to me, I asked, given all I had witnessed?

******

A few weeks later, Singy and I met for lunch at the Mount Royal Tavern.

"So" she said, after we'd placed our orders. "What's next? What you are going to do?"

"IBM's okay for now" I said. "I like not being broke all the time. I go out occasionally with a group from work. We get buzzed on whiskey sours and have expensive dinners paid for on the salesmen's expense accounts."

"What about school?"

"I'm going to continue taking part time classes. I actually like how calm my life feels right now although living at home feels harder."

"Given your Mom, I'm not surprised. Tell me more."

"I'm under constant surveillance. On one hand she says I spend too much time in my room, yet when I plan to go out there is always an inquisition - 'where are you going, who will you be with, what will you be doing, when will you be home?"

"So, what are you going to do?"

"I don't know. She even put a little chime on the front door, so that when you open the door it plays 'Bless This House'. I can't even come in at night without sounding an alarm."

Singy laughed and leaned forward in her chair grinning. "Actually, one of the reasons I wanted to meet today was to tell you about an idea I had. It might solve your problem."

She hesitated briefly before continuing. "Let's get an apartment!"

I'm sure I looked shocked but Singy continued her presentation undeterred.

"We've talked so many times about wanting to escape from our parents, but neither of us had any money. But now you have a fulltime job, so you could. I told my dad how tired I am of my daily commute and he's agreed to pay half of all expenses if I had a roommate. My mother has an attic full of perfectly decent furniture that she'd give us. So if you can't get back to school fulltime, at least you could be free. What do you think?"

I thought it was an exciting and frightening idea. The possibility of it expanded inside me in a sort of bubbly delight though I was also aware of the upset that such a decision would bring.

"Oh, Singy, that would be great. But my Mom......"

She folded her arms and fixed me with a firm stare. "You have to just do it. She's never going to like it. She wouldn't like it if you were forty years old. She controls you with that shit."

It is a vast understatement to say that my parents were unhappy with my decision. I expect that my dad would have gotten over it rather easily, but my mother became hysterical and mean. It was clear that this would not be painless. In the week before the apartment was available, I spent long hours at work, trying to avoid upset and confrontation. At night I would lie rigidly in bed, staring at the ceiling while my mother wailed and cried in the bathroom on the other side of the wall. My father's attempts to comfort her were futile. I felt horrible. I did not want her to be in such pain but realized that it wasn't something I had done but something she believed that was the source of her distress. Her rigid position was also apparent in her comments and questions.

"Are you and Singy going to hang a red light over your door?"

"What?"

"Decent young women do not get apartments. Decent young women live with their parents until they get married."

"What if I never get married?" I asked.

"Then you will always live here" she answered.

But I couldn't. I had felt constrained for so long, boxed in by rules and the expectation I be someone I wasn't. My mother's upset, anger and sense of abandonment arose from a set of fixed beliefs which seemed nearly medieval to my mind. It seemed she would rather give up our relationship rather than loosen her positions.

"If you leave" she finally said, "I will pretend that you are dead or that you were never born."

Such comments were aimed at stopping me certainly, and I knew that at any moment I could have capitulated in order to dispel her grief and create some level of peace, but I couldn't do it. I felt that if I relented, I would lose myself forever. Our church minister helped me move. My mother ignored me as I put my sparse belongings in his car. I knew I was cutting a tie that perhaps could never be righted or repaired, but I could not live the life she wanted for me.

4 Downtown Adventures and Divine

I found the apartment through a realtor, an airy second floor unit in a 19th century townhouse on tree-lined Bolton Street. The owners of the house, an older couple, lived on the first floor. Singy's brother Jack delivered the furniture Singy had chosen from their mother's attic and I arranged to move the few secondhand pieces I'd purchased for the Charles Street hideaway. I was euphoric, giddy with my newfound sense of freedom but also uneasy. I was now one hundred percent responsible for every facet of my life, and while I felt competent to handle many things, there were areas where I had little experience. I was especially nervous about finances, managing my paychecks to last through the month and paying bills on time. Now that I was estranged from my family, who could I lean on in case of mishaps and emergencies? All my friends had family they could rely on to help in hard times, but in that way, I was now truly alone.

From our apartment we had a short walk to MICA, and we also had friends in the neighborhood. Dave, Nick and Gary were still at the Marlborough. Vince Peranio, a friend I'd known since freshman year, lived on nearby Mount Royal Avenue. I visited Vince shortly after we'd gotten settled in, and I met another group of interesting friends through him. Their living room, a turreted space called the "teapot room" after Vince's series of tea pot paintings, was a marvelous jumble of dark Victorian furniture, tapestry, marble, toys, books, games, and collections of treasures of every sort, all overseen by Boogey the cat. As a group we went on numerous adventures, traveling in Jim Rathall's white bread truck. We attended festivals and art shows, played one golden afternoon in the fallen leaves of the park, and staying up all night listening to music. Singy was taking several summer classes and I'd completed enrollment for part time classes in the fall. Everything seemed to be falling neatly into place, but it wasn't long before we began to have trouble with our landlords. They complained that they could hear us walking, and suggested we put padding and rugs on the lovely hardwood floors. They spied Singy carrying a painting to class and asked that we not do artwork in the apartment. They objected to our "staying out late" (that appeared to be any time after 9PM). When at my invitation, several IBM salesmen came by with their wives to view my paintings, I was told that we had "too many visitors tromping up the stairs".

"This is like living with my mother" said Singy.

I agreed, but I'd signed a lease so couldn't see how we could move. After some thought, I remembered the name of W. Leroy

Ortel, an attorney and distance relative of my maternal grandmother. I phoned to ask his advice.

"How old are you, honey?"

"I'm twenty."

"Did anyone ask you for proof of your age when you signed the lease?"

"No. They just wanted to verify my employment."

"Well, if they didn't get proof of age and since you are not twenty-one, by Maryland law your signature on the lease is invalid. Write a note to that affect and give it to your landlords. You're free to move at any time."

We followed his instructions, tiptoeing down the stairs and sliding the note under our landlord's door. Singy found a new apartment the next day. We borrowed a truck and with the help of friends moved to apartment 8J in the Marlborough at 1701 Eutaw Place.

******

Built in 1907, this ten story Beaux-Arts building had been designed for Baltimore's wealthiest citizens. The builder's introductory brochure states that "the exterior will be of Indiana Limestone, granite, brick and terra cotta with numerous balconies, enriched with wrought iron railings". The interior would contain a "handsomely decorated cafe" and a "lobby finished in marble and relief work", hallways of marble and mosaic and elevators that were "the highest type of electric machine". A garden occupied the roof. Each suite consisted of a "foyer, parlor, dining room, kitchen, two to four bed chambers and one to two baths". The rooms were high ceilinged, and each unit included a fireplace, beautiful woodwork, and a wall safe.

Though faded, most of the original construction and layout remained in the 1960's. The lobby and hallways retained their marble and mosaic tile, wide open stairwells at the north and south side of the building were graced with ornate bronze newel posts and railings. The elevator doors were covered in heavy bronze grilles and most apartments retained the original woodwork and fireplace mantels. Our bathroom had a deep porcelain tub in which one could soak up to one's chin. There was a large pedestal sink, and the floor, walls and wainscots were of white tile. Some of the largest apartments had been reconfigured to smaller units. A wall safe in my bedroom, long plastered shut, set my fanciful nature to wonder about the previous occupants of our unit and what riches might lay forgotten in the Marlborough's thick stone walls.

Original residents included many from Baltimore's mercantile elite, most notably the art collecting sisters Claribel and Etta Cone who occupied apartments numbered 8B and 8D. The sister's wealth came from family businesses founded by their father and expanded by their brothers, from which they received generous yearly stipends.

Claribel and Etta travelled often to Europe where they spent time with friends Gertrude and Leo Stein. Leo, an art critic and collector, introduced the sisters to a number of artists including Matisse and Picasso. Their collection was compiled over many trips and included works by both of those artists as well as pieces by Cezanne, Gauguin, Degas, Van Gogh, Pissarro, Courbet and Monet. They also assembled a collection of furniture, textiles and lace as well as pieces of African, Asian and Near Eastern Art. Over the years, the sisters formed a particularly strong relationship with Matisse and continued to purchase additional pieces of his work. The eventual Cone gift bequest to Baltimore Museum of Art included over one thousand works by Matisse, the largest collection of his art in the world. [ii] On December 17, 1930, a year after Claribel's untimely death, Matisse visited Etta, his friend and patron, at her Marlborough apartment.

Thirty-six years later, I stood at my apartment door looking down the hallway to the old Cone apartments. Matisse in this building! He had ridden in the elevator just outside my door, walked down this very hall! I longed to conger up that past event, a shadow memory perhaps still present in these walls, a tesseract connection that would bypass distance as though Matisse was a mere moment from now.

Current occupants of the Marlborough spanned a wide range of ages and lifestyles. There was a klatch of older women with blue-rinsed hair who sat each afternoon in the lobby as they might have for decades. There were numerous students, a smattering of families, retirees, and singles like me who went off to work each day.

Singy and I spent our first day in the Marlborough happily arranging our new space. While visiting the drugstore on the lower level for cigarettes and snacks, we ran into Van Smith, a guy I knew from class. Van invited us to a party that evening, and his apartment

(8C) turned out to be just around the corner from ours. The party was crowded, and Van escorted us through a sea of faces, introducing us to a number of other residents, including his roommates, Steve and Lee.

"A bunch of us usually get together here most evenings" said Van in his charming Southern drawl. "You know, we just hang out, work on school projects and listen to music. Y'all are welcome to join us any time."

Singy and I did join them several times, but due to her budding romance with Dave she was not always around. As a result, I found myself spending most evenings with Van and a growing number of new friends at apartment 8C. It was essentially everyone's living room, a gathering spot, the door never locked.

One evening a plump man I'd not met before entered the foyer. He wore dark slacks and a white open-collared shirt. The sleeves were rolled up to his elbows and he shuffled across the foyer in worn loafers that seemed a size too big. A tan raincoat was draped over his arm in a stance reminiscent of a mink-draped vintage Hollywood actress posing on the red carpet.

"Honey, I'm home" he bellowed loudly. "A horrible day! My feet are killing me!"

He stopped in the doorway and lounged against the frame before launching into a very funny monologue, mocking the complaints and conversations of the suburban housewives who had been his salon clients that day. He altered his voice and pose to delineate each new speaker and the topics covered neighborhood gossip, diets, husbands, children, mothers-in-laws and how "you can't get good help anymore". He followed up with client comments made directly to him:

"Glenn honey, I'm not sure about the color. Maybe make it a bit more blond? "

"I want lots of teasing, Glenn. Some height does me wonders; don't you agree?"

"Glenn let's add more frosting. And more spray, definitely more spray! Be a darling."

"Agggghhhhhh! Bitches!" he exclaimed as he concluded his performance.

Van laughed. "Oh, stop it Bea. Such drama. Did you bring the grass?"

"See! See? More evidence! Everybody wants something from me!"

He pulled a plastic bag out of his pocket and handed it to Van, as he peered down at me as I sat on the floor with my sketch pad.

"And who are you?"

"That's Janet" said Van before I could answer. "She's our new neighbor."

"Pretty little thing" he replied distractedly, and then addressed me directly "But honey, we have to do something with your hair."

Van opened the bag which I assumed was marijuana. He pulled a pack of cigarette papers from his pocket, rolled a joint, took a drag and passed it to Glenn. Glenn also took a drag and nodded questioningly to me. I'd never smoked more than a Winston cigarette. I shook my head.

"What a serious little thing you are" Glenn said as he exhaled. "Life is for enjoying! You shouldn't say no too quickly because you might miss out on something great. It's prime grass. You'd love it."

Who was this man? I soon learned that his name was Glenn Milstead, a hairstylist from Towson; a funny sharp-witted standup comedian, who could make you laugh so hard you'd wet your pants. He could be exasperating, dramatic, unreasonable and light-fingered but also funny, good-hearted and generous, and he often gave me excellent advice.

*****

My IBM salary covered living and school expenses with a few dollars left over for fun. While I did not intend to make this work a lifetime career, for now it was my ticket to freedom. The people I worked with were largely pleasant and professional. I'd begun as a typist for a group of salesmen and engineers but was promoted to be secretary for two assistant branch managers.

The management structure at IBM was unlike any I'd experienced, as those of us working in a service capacity were overseen by an administrative manager. That meant that vacation time, sick leave, yearly reviews and salary increases were managed by someone not nearly as familiar with our performance as the people for whom we worked directly. I was fortunate in that my manager, Gene Meador, was a kind, decent and fair man.

These were boom years for the company, as their recently developed System/360 was revolutionizing the computer industry. Our office was growing rapidly and there were many significant changes, including an expansion of the administrative management team. Sadly for me, Mr. Meador was promoted to oversee a growing staff of fledgling administrators and was replaced by a newly minted manager recently elevated from the accounting department. His name was Jim, and he was a pompous little prick. In my view he was everything a manager shouldn't be. He was hostile, condescending, snottily patronizing, and had the creepy habit of eyeing people up and down as if removing their clothes. Thankfully, the bulk of my daily interactions were with sales and engineering personnel, so I was spared having to communicate with him often and avoided him as much as I could. "Keep your head down" my mother might have cautioned. "Disaster looms."

IBM was rife with rules. Salesmen laughingly told me that if they took a customer to lunch, they were never to order an alcoholic beverage, but if the customer did so, they were to join in so that the customer would feel at ease. If that were the case, however, they were forbidden to meet with any other client that day as the scent of alcohol might linger. Thus, I received a number of gleeful calls each day from salesmen informing me that they had a glass of wine, a beer or a martini and wouldn't be back in the office for the rest of the day.

There were also gloomy fashion rules. Men were required to wear dark suits (preferably black) and white shirts, the newly popular pastel dress shirts having been forbidden. Women wore conservative below-the-knee dresses, skirts or suits, nylon stockings and high heeled shoes. Women generally functioned only as support personnel with none in positions of leadership.

I have never been a "morning person" and freely admit that staying up late with my new friends in 8C did not provide improvement. But I also dealt with Baltimore's dreary never-on-time bus system, often hiking the entire distance to the office if the scheduled bus did not appear and a cab could not be found. While I was due in at 8:30, I was occasionally late - not by much, one minute or five - nothing substantial, and which I felt was more than made up for by the many times I skipped the allotted lunch hour or stayed late to complete a project. This had never been an issue for Mr. Meador, but Jim began to lie in wait by the time clock, his eyes full of scorn if I was even a minute late.

"Good morning, Miss Whittle. I'm so glad you could join us today. I certainly hope our expectation that you be at work hasn't interfered with your schedule."

Prick.

My workload varied widely due to the projects and traveling schedules of the two assistant branch managers, so on quiet days I often pitched in to help my friend Celie in the mailroom or an older gentleman whose name I now can't remember, who managed the technical library. He was a lovely man who had spent his career as a system engineer but due to a worsening vision problem had been moved to the library to await his retirement date. I saw that it was becoming difficult for him to read the reports, punch cards and material that passed his desk and he appreciated my assistance.

A few months after Jim became my manager, he summoned me to his office to tell me that due to a worsening medical condition, the librarian had decided to take his retirement earlier than planned. Surprisingly, Jim then offered me the position though his reluctance was palpable. While it was clear that he was unhappy to be making the offer, it was also equally clear that the directive had originated with upper management.

"I've no choice but to support this though I question whether it is the best solution" Jim said. "But I've been told that we need to move quickly. His retirement is effective immediately and he has recommended you as his replacement. Management feels you are the best candidate as you have familiarity with the position."

I was surprised but delighted. I had enjoyed my work in the library far more than I liked being a secretary and had hoped that I might be considered for this opportunity at some point in the future.

"The library is right next to the mailroom" cautioned Jim "so I don't want you and Celie to use this as an opportunity to talk any more than you already do."

"We don't talk a lot, Jim."

"More than is necessary to get your jobs done."

Prick.

******

Once we were settled in the new apartment and Singy had begun her relationship with Dave, she often had dinner with him, Nick and Gary in their apartment four floors below.

"Why don't you come with me tonight?" she asked. "You know everyone and Nick's cooking one of his Italian specialties."

I begged off. I had a lot of reading to do for history class, but truthfully, while I loved these older friends, they were reminders of Marty and the past. I knew I'd get over it but for now that familiar apartment was a catalyst for some unpleasant memories and didn't fit with my still embryonic plan to create a new life. I had every intention of settling down with my reading assignment but shortly after Singy left, our doorbell rang. I opened the door to find a cluster of my new friends grinning at me from the hallway. They were a rather endearing group, a patchwork of widely varying height and size, bundled up in an assortment of coats, scarves and hats purchased at army surplus or thrift stores.

"We're going for Chinese. You want to come?" said Van.

I thanked them but said that that I'd been planning on doing some reading for class.

"Oh, for heaven's sake" said Glenn. "I told you she wouldn't go. She's a little party pooper."

"I am not. I have reading to do."

"So, you'll read when you get back" he countered.

I hesitated, embarrassed to admit the truth.

"I can't" I finally said. "I don't have any money. Its two days until payday and........"

"So why didn't you just say that in the first place" bellowed Glenn. "You don't have any money. Happens to me all the time. Goodness never let a little thing like money stop you. Get your coat honey; we're going to dinner."

After dinner, with empty platters of moo-goo-gai-pan and shrimp lo mein littering the table, Glenn reached over, grabbed a handful of my shoulder length hair, and turned to Howard.

"What do you think, Harriett? What could we do with her hair?"

"It's too long" said Howard. "It weighs her down. She needs a good cut and more color. Maybe a deep auburn."

My natural hair color was a shade called strawberry blond and I wore it in typical 1960's Carnaby Street style, straight with a center part, sometimes tying it back into a ponytail.

"Long hair is easy" I said. "I don't have to style it. And when I'm painting, I can just pull it back out of the way."

Glenn rolled his eyes.

"Anyway" I continued "I've been told that not much can be done with my hair because it is too fine."

"Who said that?" asked Glenn.

"The owner of a salon I used to go to. Barry at 'Le Triolet'.

"Barry! Pffft! I know him. He's not as good as me. And anyway, don't you want some cute boy to think you look good?"

"Not particularly".

"Can you stand it?" Glenn said, folding his arms across his chest. "Not particularly" she said. "Such a liar. You have to play up your assets, honey. I'm going to work on you."

******

The IBM library spanned two rooms. The first held my desk and several locked cabinets containing binders of proprietary information for which I held the keys. Company regulations stated that only salesmen and system engineers were to be given access to this material and the cabinets were to remain locked until such requests were made. Materials in the binders could not be copied or taken from the room and it was my responsibility to watch each user for compliance and to return the binder to its shelf and relock the cabinets.

The second room contained a floor to ceiling bin system housing multiple copies of manuals related to the company's various machines and systems. I regularly placed orders with IBM's printing facility in order to keep the bins supplied, but also to fulfill requests from the staff and to place large orders for shipment directly to customers. Orders included manuals as well as the popular THINK desk plaques available in multiple languages. I took some of those plaques home and hung them on the wall near my workspace: THINK in French, Italian, Gaelic, Hebrew, Persian, Korean, Japanese and Thai.

If I thought enough, I reasoned, maybe I could figure a way to escape this place and go back to school.

Jim continued to slink about the office, draped in self-importance and ever on the lookout for something to criticize. He would pop into the library to complain about things he didn't understand, once questioning the necessity of the locked cabinets, another time berating me because a specific manual was out of stock. While he suggested that I had been remiss in placing the necessary order, the facts were otherwise. IBM's printing facility in Mechanicsburg had completely exhausted their inventory, the result being that every IBM office on the east coast had had their requests backordered for weeks, a fact known to all in the room but him. It seemed clear that he was searching for some way to justify demoting or firing me.

One morning, soaking wet from travel through a fierce rainstorm, I dashed up the stairs to find Jim lurking by the time clock once again.

"Good morning, Miss Whittle. I'm so glad you could join us. I hope we haven't inconvenienced you by expecting you to come to work today."

"Everyone's late once in a while" I said. "It's raining really hard. Things happen."

"But they happen to you, Miss Whittle, far more frequently than they've ever happened to me."

He folded his arms, admiring his manicure. "You may wonder

why you don't get a raise, and here you have a reason. Lateness. Not good at all."

"It's not as if I'm late all the time, Jim. And I frequently work through lunch or stay late."

"That is not the point. I don't see how you can expect to do well here if you are not willing to follow the rules. Now you had better get to your desk. You have wasted my time and are now at least five minutes late in beginning your work."

Droopy and wet, I slumped against the wall.

Prick.

It wasn't as though I hadn't imagined a more forceful response to Jim's harassment, but I simply did not have the courage. I'd been raised in an environment where women, particularly young women, did not stand against men in power. He had the authority and the power to hurt my life, and I could not give him a reason to fire me. Money was tight and I had no reserves, no family to rely on for help, so losing my job would be a disaster.

I did wonder about his reference to raises, but for obvious reasons it was a conversation I was loath to approach. Another IBM rule stated that salary was not to be discussed with other staff, so I really couldn't ask anyone's opinion for to do so could result in dismissal.

Sales and system engineers praised my work. The library, which had been badly out of date, was now current and functioning to their and the customer's needs. Jim, however, seemed to have disliked me from the start. I didn't know what about me produced this reaction, but it seemed clear that I had to be careful.

******

"So" said Glenn as he plopped down next to me on the couch one evening not long after we met, "what's the story with you? You're from Baltimore?"

I said yes but offered no detail. In truth, I'd purposefully avoided any mention of Highlandtown or East Baltimore ever since starting classes at MICA. Most of the people I met downtown seemed far cooler than I and many came from more sophisticated, educated or wealthier backgrounds. In many parts of Baltimore, the Highlandtown area was disparaged as a tacky uncultured place, and I did not want to provide evidence for my being as bush-league provincial as I feared I was.

"You're a part time student at MICA now" continued Glenn, but Van said you were full time before" Glenn asked. "How'd that happen?"

This was another subject I usually skirted successfully, but I hadn't learned yet that Glenn never dropped things easily. He continued prodding for an answer.

"It's a long story" I finally said. "My boyfriend flunked out and I didn't have the money to continue. We decided to get jobs and save money so we could get married, but it didn't work out."

"You mean he dumped you".

I glared at him over my cigarette. "Yes. He dumped me. You just say whatever you think, don't you?"

"He usually does" said Van as he joined us on the couch.

"Oh, let me tell you the rest" said Glenn. "You were sad. It had seemed so perfect, so you started asking yourself why it happened and what's wrong with you that it did. Am I right?"

I didn't answer because it was true.

Glenn said that people who say they are committed to a something in the future but who don't deliver are just not worth your time. "They are too much work, honey. If they don't want it, you can't want it enough for them. So what you really should be saying is 'Wow, I dodged a fucking bullet! There must be something seriously wrong with that asshole if he left me'."

Van and I laughed. Glenn lit a cigarette and then continued. "I once had a lover who cheated on me. He didn't think I knew, but I did. We had a gorgeous apartment. So, one morning after we both left for work, I went back with a truck and I stripped that place bare. I took everything – the furniture, television, dishes, my clothes, his clothes -- I even removed the doorknobs. And I left a note which said 'God giveth and God taketh away and so does Bea.' And then I went on with my life, with being a star! I know people don't believe it when I say I'm a star, but I am. And one day they'll know it too."

Over time and numerous conversations, Glenn and I learned

that we had many things in common. There were similarities in our childhood experiences, and we'd both felt the constraints of our parent's standards and views. We'd been outsiders who had difficulty being accepted and had endured a good bit of teasing and emotional abuse. Glenn's experience was far worse than mine as he'd endured several physical attacks and beatings. He said that mean people can hurt you physically, but what's worse is the hurt you feel inside.

"They say mean things and you start to believe them, so you have to stop listening. You have to say who you're going to be instead of giving in to their predictions. Fuck them."

Glenn was easy to talk with, and while I found that he could also be brutally frank, there was a vulnerability and a kindness there that people who did not know him likely never saw.

8C was, of course, the place where I also met John Waters and several of his other stars. I was talking with Glenn and Van one evening when the front door opened and a slim young man with dark shoulder length hair entered the apartment. He was accompanied by another man with white blood hair and dark glasses, and two women, one very glamorously attired. Everyone seemed to know them.

"Oh, do come in" said Glenn. "And I hope you've brought some grass with you."

"That's John" said Van leaning over my shoulder. He's a filmmaker. And Bonnie, Mink and David are his stars."

"But I'm the biggest star, darling" added Glenn. "No one is so divine as Divine."

"That's his stage name" explained Van, noticing my confusion.

Bonnie posed dramatically in the doorway and then did a runway walk and turn as well as any model. I was in awe of her appearance. Her platinum hair, dark eye makeup, and vintage clothing, all sparkly silver and fur, were glamorously reminiscent of the original blond bombshell, Jean Harlow. It was as if she had stepped out of the black and white films I'd sneak downstairs to watch on late night television when I was in high school.

Who knew it was possible to have such fun with clothes? My clothes were ordinary and IBM safe. I had no idea what to wear or what would work for me. I was equally inept regarding hairstyles and makeup. I was envious of women who could look so flawless.

"That's what you need" said Glenn leaning towards me.

"What?"

"A little style, sugar. You could wear outfits like that."

"Mmmm, no. I'm too fat."

"Who said that? The jerk you almost married? He was an ass, but he was right about your clothes" Glenn said as he tugged at my shirt. "And you need a hairstyle. And makeup."

"I wear makeup."

"Not enough. Don't be a little bitch. You could look way better than you do."

While John and his entourage didn't live in the Marlborough, they dropped by 8C frequently. In a letter containing reminiscences from those years, Greg wrote:

"One time I went upstairs, and John Waters was filming "Eat Your Makeup" in George's apartment. It was quite a scene, very party-like. Actually, every time we went up there, there was always a party. I might be an extra in that film which I've never seen. John Waters and his entourage were around the Marlborough a lot. It was always so cool; John was our Andy Warhol. They always walked by with the idea that they were on a mission. A very colorful group of people."

Later in life when I've mentioned those long-ago Marlborough days, people have asked if I ever spoke with John about my East Baltimore background. I didn't, of course, for the same reason I withheld that information from Glenn. I was embarrassed to be from a place people considered to be blue collar and uncool. I've sometimes wondered, however, if my experiences would have been useful to him as he envisioned my Highlandtown world. I remember John as being quiet, not the funny and articulate man he is today. At the time I had the impression that he was always thinking and observing, but, of course, it may have been a misinterpretation. We were, after all, frequently stoned.

Life in the Marlborough continued to be fun and deliciously free. Glenn dubbed our group "The Fucknutty Family" and gave many of us a nickname. While he answered to Glenn, he more often referred to himself as Bea or Aunt Bea in addition to his stage name of Divine. Some of the nicknames we went by are listed below though they often changed on a whim:

Van Smith (Stumpi)

George Tamsitt (Spider Lady)

Steve (Mr. Nice)

Howard Gruber (Harriet or Galaxy Gruber)

Paul (Uncle Paul)

Chuck (Smokey the Silver Flash)

Barbara (Batty)

Bonnie (Boom-Boom or Ruby-Pearl-Diamond)

Debbie (Go-Go)

Michael (Miss Mess)

Me (Twiggy, Mama Cass or Miss Melanie)

Others in our group who somehow escaped Glenn's nicknaming included Lee Hoffman, Greg, Kit Throssell, Bob McCormack, and David Lehman. As mentioned, we were often joined by John Waters and David Lochary; and sometimes by Pat Moran, Sue Lowe, Bonnie (Mary Vivian) Pearce and Mink Stole.

******

Though life in the Marlborough continued to be fun, I was increasingly unhappy at work. Jim continued to be his obnoxious creepy self and I still had not received any salary increase. With our next payday nearly a week away, I sat down to figure how to make my few dollars last until Friday. I could walk to work, a long hike but I would save bus fare. I usually skipped breakfast, so that wasn't an issue. A 25-cent coffee from the machine each morning would total $1.25. Cigarettes were thirty-five cents a pack for another $1.75. I spent the balance at the grocery store, purchasing a small loaf of white bread and some cheese to make lunch sandwiches and a small tray of chicken parts, two potatoes and two carrots with which I made an uninspiring stew that I ate for four nights in a row. Yes, I could have asked for help, but it is wearisome and embarrassing to be the most broke in a group where nearly everyone is.

The next afternoon, I approached Celie on the subject of salaries, asking her if there was some time range for expecting raises. She said that she usually got one on her yearly anniversary and if I hadn't there must be some mistake.

"Maybe you ought to talk to Jim about it" she said.

It was unlikely that I would do that, but some weeks later an opportunity for discussion arose. Business was booming, we were all extremely busy and it seemed the company couldn't hire people fast enough. One day Jim informed me that there had been several new administrative hires, one a young man who would function as my assistant. He went on to fuss about where he would seat this person, given that my office was not large enough to accommodate another desk.

"There is no room here" he sighed. "There might be space in the mail room, of course, but that is completed inappropriate for a young man moving onto the management track."

Management track? My assistant?

"Is that something that I could be considered for, Jim?"

"A woman? Do you see any women in management here, Miss Whittle? Or anywhere else for that matter? You've already moved from typist to secretary to librarian, a position that has always been held by a man. Further than many women go."

"But..."

"You can hardly expect the same opportunities, Miss Whittle. He will have a family to support one day and will need a good job. You'll probably get married and have a man take care of you."

"If he is my assistant but also a management trainee, does that mean he will make a larger salary?"

He did not address my question but slipped quickly into his usual combative mode.

"You haven't been discussing salaries, have you? You know that is a serious infraction. Completely against company policy."

I thought of Glenn and his now oft repeated exhortation that I should stand up for myself.

"No, I haven't" I said firmly, steeling myself for an uncomfortable conversation, "but I have been wondering about mine...."

"Your salary is well within guidelines, Miss Whittle" he snapped. "And please remember that a man's salary reflects the fact that he will always have more financial responsibility."

"But you said he was single and so am I. We must have the same expenses, and I've been with the company longer."

He straightened his starched cuffs and turned towards the door.

"I'm terminating this conversation and will not discuss it further. Now, if you'll excuse me, I have a meeting to attend." And with that he turned and left the room. I knew full well that if he had the balls to do it, he would gladly move me to a corner somewhere and give my desk to my "assistant". It was likely that only the possible rolled eyes and questions from the sales and engineering staff that kept him from doing so.

*****

For weeks on end Glenn continued to nag me about my appearance, groaning over my ponytailed hair or lack of eye makeup. I resisted his prodding, fearing any changes he might have in mind would be too drastic for IBM. I didn't doubt that improvements could be made, but I worried that his ideas might be too edgy. Ultimately, he enrolled Van into his project which eased my fears. Van was a fashion major, and he understood my needing to fit into the business world and assured me they would do nothing extreme. Glenn was delighted. He'd been bent on having his way, and to be honest, I was curious.

I now found myself the beneficiary of their expertise as they took on being my personal stylists. Glenn brought books and magazines from his salon that illustrated a variety of hairstyles, all far more stylish than my current cut which Glenn referred to as "the hippie look". He also brought a board of hair swatches in a multitude of shades and held them one by one against my face.

"Hmm. Harriett was right" he said. "This auburn does great things for your skin."

I curled up my nose a bit, thinking it was far too dark.

"Nonsense" he responded. "Your hair already had red in it. We'll just be accentuating it a bit."

I soon had a Vidal Sassoon inspired chin length angled bob in a rich medium auburn. Van, with a better eye than I, took me on a number of shopping excursions, choosing outfits that I would have breezed right by.

"You can't go by how they look on the hanger darlin, you've got to try them on" he said.

And try them on I did. We searched the sale racks of the grand downtown department stores: Hutzler Brothers, Hoschild-Kohn, Stewart's, The Hecht-May Company and Brager Gutman. We mined the Nearly New Shoppe, a thrift store on Howard Street run by the Women's Board of Johns Hopkins Hospital. Here I purchased several items, including a 1940's era black lamb's wool jacket with padded shoulders, a black satin cocktail dress, and a pale peach silk kimono embroidered with peonies and birds.

Van became my makeup artist. I learned to apply shadow, liner, lashes and blush and was soon scouting the makeup counters at Hutzler's for new products. For fun outings, the makeup grew more playful or exotic. Once, before we attended a dance at MICA, Van was inspired to paint one side of my face with flowers. He'd gotten the idea from a cover of one of the high-end fashion magazines - either Vogue or Bazaar - where the model's face had been painted in that way, beginning at the hairline and curving downward to the earlobe and branching out onto the cheekbone. It was a long and tedious process during which Van often growled "sit still" "don't blink" "stop grousing" and "no, you can't have a cigarette until I'm finished!" It was a showstopper look though that garnered much attention. I felt more glamorous and sophisticated than my East Baltimore self would have ever hoped to be.

As I walked across the dance floor that evening, a petite young woman in a white mini dress approached to speak to me. It took a moment for me to realize that it was my friend Howard in drag and looking adorable. I smiled as I watched all the straight guys trailing after him throughout the evening. They hadn't a clue.

Although Glenn was working as a stylist at the James Hair Salon in Towson, his confidence in his future stardom was intriguing. He couldn't comprehend how I could tolerate the brassbound environment of IBM and endorsed full rebellion against Jim though he didn't seem to comprehend that dismissal and a loss of income would be the likely result.

"Then leave. You should get back in school fulltime anyway."

Bless him, he regularly encouraged me to return to school fulltime though he failed to appreciate the finer details such as how I would pay for tuition and rent. I learned in short order that Glenn wasn't particularly realistic about money, though I was likely at the opposite end of the spectrum -- too practical, too cautious and risk adverse.

"I can't see how I could do that" I responded. "I don't have any money."

"That you can't see a way doesn't mean there isn't one" he insisted. "If you keep thinking like that you'll always be stuck."

"Well, it isn't that I don't want to get back to school fulltime. I hope to be able to at some point in the future."

"Hope? You're always hoping. You hope too much. You hoped about that jerk you almost married. You hope you'll get your degree one day. You hope that little fuck at IBM will give you a raise. You can hope forever, and nothing will change. One of my clients told me about a guy she saw on a talk show. He said that what you believe predicts your future, and I think he was right."

I knew I had made progress, but Glenn was correct that in some ways I was not moving forward. And while he didn't succeed in convincing me to quit my job, he continued to encourage me to indulge my new free-spirited bent. Loosen up. Have fun. Be confident. Stand up for yourself. Those were his mantras and ones I was slowly able to absorb.

******

The hippie counterculture and New Age movements of the 1960's brought with it a renewed interest in astrology. Everyone seemed to have a passing understanding of the personality traits assigned to individual zodiac signs as well as which signs they were supposedly compatible with. It all seems a bit silly now, but it wasn't at all unusual for new acquaintances to pose the question "what's your sign?" shortly after being introduced. Eventually Glenn and I got around to that conversation and were surprised to find that we were both Libras. We also discovered that we had been born only four days apart and in the same hospital.

"That's why we get along" Glenn said, laughing. "We probably already met in the nursery."

I rolled my eyes in response.

"Don't laugh. It's possible" he said. "My mother told me they used to keep mothers and babies in the hospital for a week or longer back then. We're Astro-twins! "

Our group was fluid, with some or all of us present at any given time. We listened to music, watched the Smother's Brother Show and Rowen and Martin's Laugh-In, appreciative of their sharp social and political satire that was, like us, anti-war and anti-establishment. We smoked weed and hashish. Along with the horde of students in the neighborhood and inspired by Donovan's folk-rock song "Mellow Yellow", we stripped the local grocery store of bananas, baking their skins in search of a cheap hallucinogen. We saw movies at the many downtown theatres, attended gallery shows and the yearly outdoor art festival that circled the reservoir at Druid Hill Park[iii]. Druid Hill, established in 1860 and spanning seven hundred and forty-five acres, is one of the first large public parks in America. The reservoir, completed in 1871 is fifty-five acres in size, and hundreds of artists displayed their work around the periphery with crowds upward of forty thousand enjoying the show.

We went to dinner at now long-gone iconic Baltimore restaurants such as Nate's and Leon's landmark deli on North Avenue. In celebration of his birthday, George purchased one of their mammoth strawberry cakes that we nibbled on for days. Stoned and hungry, we trekked downtown to Connelly's Seafood on pier 5 for crab cakes and seafood platters. Connelly's was old time Baltimore, a restaurant that Fred Rasmussen of the Baltimore Sun later described as that "rattletrap seafood venue that defied the march of time and Inner Harbor development"[iv]. Another favorite was Mee Jung Lo's[v] on Mulberry Street where we often dined on eggrolls, wonton soup and shared platters of orange chicken, spareribs, and shrimp lo mein. The lone waitress, a woman of American Indian heritage named Irene, screamed orders to the kitchen in Cantonese. It was not unusual to wait for a table there, the line sometimes stretching down the narrow staircase onto the street. Customers ranged from students to middle-aged couples in formal dress stopping for an early dinner on their way to the theatre. When money was tight or when there was a lot of schoolwork to complete, we opted for burgers or chicken from the original Gino's on North Avenue, subs from Harley's on McMechen Street, or potato chips and candy bars from our street level pharmacy.

All of our activities seemed overlaid with music -- Motown for sure, as well as folk, pop and rock: Joan Baez, Janis Ian, Jefferson Airplane, Buffalo Springfield, Simon & Garfunkel, Judy Collins, The Association, The Who, The Byrds, Paul Revere and The Raiders, The Beatles, Donovan, The Mamas and the Papas, The Bee Gees, Steppenwolf, The Doors, and many more.

I had spent most of my life submerged in cautions, clinging to safety in order to avoid imagined threats and dangers. That sort of mindset is a killer of aliveness and often had me plodding through life with low expectations and little freedom or fun. My new friends were not run by such cautions. They had a large focus on fun and adventure, a point of view that Glenn once called "joyful extravagance". While we did not have much money, we were able to have some satisfying and grand times that still live in my memory today.

I felt I could be myself with my new friends. My world had become roomier, more ample, and I felt accepted and sufficient and somehow strengthened by their friendship. Our group became a family to me. "It was" said one friend, "the first time for many of us that we were not the odd man out".

*****

Although I made certain that my parents had my contact information, I did not hear from them, so I assumed my mother had declared me dead as she had threatened. The most difficult time was Christmas. All my out-of-state friends returned home for the long holiday, and local friends were probably with their families. I might have arranged something I suppose, but I did not think about it nor plan how I would spend that day. I also did not anticipate how that day would feel.

Initially all was festive. There were Christmas decorations everywhere and a staff luncheon at work. Singy and I put up a small tree in our living room, decorating it with our costume jewelry. I began to sense my aloneness on Christmas Eve, so I distracted myself by going shopping. Downtown Baltimore was always lavishly decorated at Christmas, the streets festooned with banners, greenery, ornaments and lights. Sidewalk vendors selling roasted chestnuts, pine boughs, holly and mistletoe gave the streets a festive air. The four major department stores filled their display windows with elaborate scenes including animated figures of Santa, Mrs. Claus, elves and reindeer. There were smoke puffing Lionel trains winding through miniature snowy villages, fantasy castles, nativity scenes with shepherds and wise men, stuffed animals, toys, dolls and expensively dressed mannequins. The traffic was heavy that evening and there were still many shoppers in the stores. I had dinner and made several purchases before heading back to the Marlborough. When I arrived, I found that Singy, who had gone home to Westminster several days before, had returned to leave several parcels for me under the tree. While I appreciated her kindness, I felt a sudden pang of sadness at seeing them, as my family, so important in all my Christmases past, had apparently not given me a thought. I pictured past celebrations at my parent's home. My mother always put a lot of energy into Christmas, decorating the entire house and baking numerous cookies and cakes. There was a real tree, poinsettias, pine boughs and wreaths as well as an antique creche. There would be a midnight Christmas Eve service at church, followed by a present exchange and a turkey dinner with all the trimmings on Christmas Day. Other family members would be present, of course. I wondered what explanation would be given regarding my absence. The Marlborough was unusually quiet, and it did feel strange to be completely alone on a holiday usually packed with activity and family. I don't remember what I did or ate, but I survived.

While I had no communication from my parents, I did, on occasion, hear from Singy's parents and that sometimes required some verbal maneuvers that had me dance between truth and lies.

"My father is coming to town to take me to dinner" announced Singy one evening "and you have to go with us."

I thought my presence would be an intrusion on a family visit but Singy was insistent. "You have to go" she said. "If you are there, he will behave himself. He won't give me a hard time or ask all the embarrassing questions he is sure to ask otherwise."

Thus, I had a number of dinners at some of Baltimore's finer restaurants that neither I nor any other of my friends could have afforded: Marconi's, with its crystal chandeliers, traditional French menu and tuxedoed waiters; the expensive and exclusive Chesapeake restaurant serving local seafood; and Velleggia's in Little Italy where Mayor Thomas D'Alesandro Jr. (Nancy Pelosi's father) often held court. Mr. Tevis was a charming and entertaining host and the embarrassing questions that Singy feared were always avoided.

I did not fare as well with Mrs. Tevis. Like my mother, she seemed to be constantly looking for some suspected impropriety, some way that Singy might not be aligning with her rather old-fashioned sense of decorum, which, in fact, she was not. Once she was involved with Dave, Singy often spent the night at his apartment. One morning, incredibly early, the insistent ringing of our phone awakened me long before my alarm clock was scheduled to go off. In the darkness I staggered sleepily to the phone to discover that the caller was Mrs. Tevis, asking to speak with Singy. I had to think fast.

"Oh, I'm sorry Mrs. Tevis; she's not here. She went out early on a photo shoot for class."

After a polite but brief conversation I promised to let Singy know of her call. As I turned to replace the phone's receiver, I saw dimly through the window the gray drab and rainy morning. It was raining hard, so hard in fact, that no sane person would be attempting a photography excursion. Since Westminster was less than an hour away, I could be certain that Mrs. Tevis knew I was lying although her well-bred and aristocratic Southern self would have never said so.

I quickly pulled on some clothes and dashed down to Dave's, to tell Singy of her mother's call and my apparent slip-up. She was unflustered.

"She's just spying on me" she said. "I'll call her later."

I remember being stunned that she could be so sassy when I would have scurried around trying to fix things or cover them up. I apparently still had a lot to learn. I certainly saw similarities between

Mrs. Tevis and my mother. She expected her daughter to follow all the rules for female behavior set in stone for generations. But we clearly weren't going to.

******

A downside to life as a female office worker has always been the lecherous male. Most of the salesmen and engineers at IBM were decently behaved. And then there was Al. Al was handsome in a sleazy Mediterranean sort of way. He was intrigued by the fact that I attended art school as he had a particular interest in nude models. I would sigh and brace myself for an uncomfortable conversation each time Al entered the library. He would sit on the edge of my desk and inquire about school, always asking if he could come to my class "for a look". While he didn't make a lecherous move towards me, these conversations were awkward and embarrassing, but I had no idea how to make him stop. One afternoon Al wandered into the library and sat once again on the edge of my desk, thumbing through a manual he'd just removed from the shelf.

"You never talk to me about that school of yours" he said. "I thought you were going to invite me to one of your classes."

"I didn't know you were interested" I said, as I uncomfortably shuffled papers on my desk.

"Now you know I'm interested" he answered. "You were supposed to let me know when you were going to have a model."

Suddenly, in a flash, I saw the possibility for terminating these creepy conversations.

"Well..." I said, "I have class tonight. We're having the same model as last week."

"So I can come down?"

"I don't imagine anyone would stop you."

"Where?"

"MICA's main building on Mt. Royal Avenue. We're in the large studio on the third floor."

Al arrived just as class was beginning, standing out like a sore thumb in his IBM business suit. Students surrounded the dais in the center of the room, busily setting up their workstations. Through the jungle of easels, I could see Al in the doorway, standing on tiptoe in order to have a better view. It couldn't have been more perfect if I had choreographed it myself. The model was on the dais, still robed and facing away from the door. I watched as the model's satin robe dropped to the floor and Al's facial expression chanced from anticipation to surprise and finally to annoyance as he focused on the ponytailed guy in a jock strap striking his first pose on the dais. One must have little victories. Glenn would be proud. Al left me alone after that.

******

While I spent most of my free time with my friends in 8C, I also stayed in touch with Vince and his tribe. They moved from the Mount Royal apartment to another only several blocks south of us on Eutaw Street. It was a first-floor apartment in what had once been a really grand townhome. The space still retained much of the original detail including marvelous woodwork, tall, shuttered windows and huge pocket doors.

We once attended a Mamas and the Papas concert at the Baltimore Civic Center, but being mostly broke, we couldn't often afford such expenditures. We hung out, mostly just talking, some of us dabbling in folk music, and often sharing a few joints. On one such occasion someone started talking about bread – "real bread' he called it, not that flabby, fluffy stuff from the A & P store but the sort of bread his grandmother used to bake and that he remembered eating warm from the oven. Weed is a great appetite enhancer, and we were all quickly longing for such a loaf. I mentioned that I had baked bread in the past and that we could make some if I still had the recipe.

"Can't you remember?" someone asked.

I wasn't sure that I could, and a quick look into Vince's kitchen cabinets, revealed that he didn't have any measuring utensils either. Perhaps, I thought, I could approximate the amounts I needed but it would be pure guesswork. Eventually our bread fantasies dragged us from our seats to put on our coats and trek several blocks to the A&P. Stoned, and thus easily distracted, we roamed the aisles like unherdable cats, finally locating the yeast, flour, sugar, cinnamon and butter. I don't believe I've ever had a yeast bread rise as well as that batch did. We used every acceptable baking utensil in Vince's kitchen, forming loaves and cinnamon buns, the dough spiraled around a filling of butter, sugar and cinnamon. We baked them in batches, filling our stomachs with this relatively cheap carbohydrate feast.

It seems remarkable to me now that I had been friends with these two distinct groups of creative people, but somehow never had the opportunity or thought to introduce them. How wonderful that they would later meet and work together in successful screen careers. That is so Baltimore, or at least the Baltimore that once was.

******

Our apartment rent increased, and I was really feeling the financial pinch. IBM paid bi-weekly, and Singy often covered our bills until my paycheck cleared the bank. Living expenses had become an uncomfortable and repetitious juggling act that frequently had me feeling as though I was dangling near disaster.

"I'm starving. Let's go to dinner" said Glenn.

"Can't. I've only got a few bucks until payday."

"Oh please! You say that all the damn time. Why don't you tell them you have to have a raise?"

"This is not the James Hair Salon, Glenn. It is tight-assed IBM. And trust me, it would not go well. I've told you before what a bastard my boss is."

"Well if they don't give you a raise soon, you are going to have to do something. It's not as though they don't have plenty of money. Meanwhile let's get Chinese. I'll pay."

There were a number of outings where Glenn generously footed the bill. Once he, George and I went to a female impersonator extravaganza at a theatre on Pennsylvania Avenue. I was unaware of the history of the venue at that time but realize now that it was the old Royal Theatre which stood at 1329 Pennsylvania Avenue, a building steeped in African American musical history. It was here that Ethel Waters and Pearl Bailey made their debuts. The Royal had presented performances by a long list of legends: Louis Armstrong, Fats Waller, Duke Ellington, Etta James, Nat King Cole, Louis Jordan, The Platters, The Temptations and The Supremes. With its golden age passed, the theatre was used to screen movies and for special events. The show we witnessed was a competitive pageant and talent show, with a succession of participants in dazzling costumes, outrageous hairstyles and extravagant makeup. Glenn was in heaven; George and I were well entertained.

Weeks later Singy presented another possible Pennsylvania Avenue adventure, this time with Scotty, a friend who we'd known since our freshman year. Scotty was African American, perhaps in his late forties, and worked as a custodian at MICA. At some point he'd spoken of a gambling hall he frequented and Singy, ever curious, begged to be taken along. He'd agreed, and she now wanted me to go with them. I thought it sounded dangerous on a number of levels, not the least of which was the possibility of being arrested since such operations were clearly illegal. As usual, Singy was relentless and I finally agreed. We met Scotty on a Friday evening when the sidewalks of Pennsylvania Avenue were crowded with people heading into the weekend. As we walked down the street, I was struck by how many men greeted Scotty with a deferential "good evening Mr. Scott". Several young men stepped off the curb to make way for him with a respectful greeting.

"What do I not know about Scotty" I mused. "Maybe he is Mafioso."

Scotty led us into a small store – a confectionary or small grocery as I remember, a darkened space with a relatively low inventory on the wooden shelves. A hulking man with large Bunyanesque muscles stood with his arms crossed near the counter. He did not speak but nodded to Scotty as we passed by, heading to a door at the far end of the room.

When Scotty opened that door, we stepped from the darkness of that small store into a much larger and brightly lit space that was bursting with people, noise and music. It was a real casino; there were tables for poker, Blackjack and craps, large clacking numbered betting wheels, a bar, and live music. The volume of the conversation and music dropped abruptly to a low hum as nearly all the people turned to stare at the two white girls standing at the entrance. Everyone recovered quickly, however, and Scotty was soon leading us around the room, introducing us to people and explaining the games that Singy had wanted to learn. It was an experience that you would not have predicted when Scotty opened that door in the back of that worn old store. So much goes on in this city and even more in the wider world I thought, about which I didn't have a clue.

This photo was taken of Singy, Scotty and myself at my
21st birthday party in 1966.

******

I was feeling increasingly grumpy at work. My "assistant" was
as dumb as a rock but possessed a penis which qualified him to earn a
larger salary. A rosebud in a cheap vase appeared on my desk for
"National Secretaries Day". I found it condescending and fought the
urge to throw it across the room. The rigid dress code felt increasingly
oppressive. I'd been pleased when the new shorter stacked heels came
into fashion, because I did a considerable amount of both walking and
ladder climbing through the day and standard high heels left me feeling
like a cripple by noon. Jim made it clear that he disapproved of my
new shoes and told me to never wear them again. They were, he said,
"unprofessional" and "wholly inappropriate for the office". So office
appropriate high heels, along with my more conventional clothing took
up on one side of my closet while studio wear and colorful fun outfits
selected by Glenn and Van dominated the other. In almost every way
I was living a schizophrenic sort of life - restrained, conventional and

professional at work, a bohemian, avant-garde, fun loving artist with my friends.

Since I could only do part time classes, I found that my artwork was enriched by Singy's full time experience. We had frequent conversations about the direction of our work as well as class content, instructors and assignments. One of her professors advised their class to keep a journal in which they recorded thoughts about their work as well as inspirations and ideas for future projects. I loved the idea and began one of my own in an old-fashioned ledger journal purchased at an office supply store. In it I recorded comments about my current classes, the themes of my paintings and ideas or sketches for new work. It became in part a diary, including comments on life issues, conversations with friends, quotes I'd found meaningful, as well as personal and creative introspections and poems. That journal is, of course, why I can remember so much of the past as clearly as I do. In colored markers the journal also includes my "IBM poems

You didn't know

when I was there

among you pretending

to be what you

thought I was that

I was really me and

only fooling you

***

Did they say I shouldn't

Be sitting here till dawn

writing

to keep up with my head

and smoking too many again

when

tomorrow I'll be tired and coughing

and didn't I know it was going to be

a straight day

Singy, for all her playful and high-strung ways, took her painting very seriously. She was completely committed to her work and it was inspiring to see the pieces she produced in class. In the Marlborough she began a series of paintings based on old family photographs from the 1930s, the first of which was done on the large ochre window shade in my bedroom.

After the earlier upheavals I'd experienced, I was excited to be refocused on school, and Singy's creativity urged mine forward. My drawings and paintings at this time were of the human form. Inspired by life drawing classes and the work of Larry Rivers I began painting female figures, some mythological, their bodies fleshy and voluptuous, equally a celebration of their sensuality and the fat, oily, lushness of paint. I wanted to paint nudes that were classical in attitude if not in mathematical perfection, nudes that were uninhibited and stood with confidence. These were paintings I could not have done in my parent's home. The subject would not have been approved of, nor would it have been logistically possible to transport my large canvases by bus or cab from East Baltimore. From the Marlborough, it was a doable walk to class.

One night I was alone in the apartment, listening to music as I worked on a canvas that was going especially well. It was my interpretation of Venus rising from the sea, her pale skin and the peachy shading of the shell rising behind her worked in oils with the old master's Flemish medium of Jacques Maroger.[vi] As I worked, my stereo dropped the next record, a Simon and Garfunkel album. As the duo launched into "Bridge Over Troubled Waters" it occurred to me that the lyrics mapped onto my experience and it seemed as if they were singing just to me.

"Sail on Silver Girl

Sail on by

Your time has come to shine

All your dreams are on their way

See how they shine"

How far I had come from the East Baltimore girl I once was. I had escaped the limits of the world I grew up in and the narrow role in life laid out for me. While I had made mistakes and had disappointments, I had survived, and I felt that my life was now wholly mine. I would complete my education. I had an apartment, friends, interesting classes, a job, and time to find and be myself. I was rich. I WAS the silver girl.

******

John Waters had just finished his first 16 mm film entitled "Eat Your Makeup", and we were preparing our stylish selves for the world premier to be held in the basement of Emmanuel Episcopal Church on Cathedral Street. Glenn was excited. This was his second starring role in one of John's films, and he saw this as part of the progression that would establish him as the star he knew he was. George drove us downtown in his new yellow convertible.

"Stop at Leon's on the way, George" exclaimed Glenn. "I've got to see somebody. It will only take a minute."

George sighed. From experience, he knew that "it will only take a minute" could easily expand to some unknown quantity of time. Glenn often had less sense of reality around time than he did about money.

"We shouldn't stop" George said. "You always make us late."

"I'm telling you it will only take a minute" said Glenn impatiently. "Just park right in front and leave the engine running. Janet, come with me."

He got out of the front seat, folding it forward so I could exit the back and put out his hand to me. I hesitated. I knew that Leon's was a male gay bar and I thought I'd feel uncomfortably out of place.

"I'll just wait here with George" I said.

"Oh, for God sake, just come with me" he said, standing there with his hand offered to me.

"It's a gay bar" I said.

"I'm well aware of that" Glenn laughed. "No one will bother you. You're a girl."

"Go with him" said George. "You can make sure he gets out in time. Otherwise he's going to make us late."

"Oh, alright" I said as Glenn grabbed my hand, tugging me from the back seat.

We walked the remaining few steps to Leon's entry door. Glenn reached out for the doorknob, but as he did, the door was pushed open from the inside. The person opening the door now stood frozen and speechless in the doorway. It seemed that we stood there for a long time though it was likely only seconds. Then the man mumbled something unintelligible, turned and hurried down the street.

"Who the fuck was that??" shrieked Glenn.

"My boss" I answered.

Glenn, never shy about expressing himself, bellowed loudly. "Oh my god! That's the little bastard you're always complaining about?" he asked as he collapsed into laughter.

"Oh, honey, oh my" Glenn said as he quieted down." Not a problem for you, of course, but clearly one for him!"

Well, it was funny.

But I did worry over how this would translate when I returned to work on Monday. Jim had power and I had none. He already seemed to hate me, and now surely felt compromised. Lifestyles outside of what 1960's IBM considered proper could cause individuals serious problems, and I knew of several instances involving affairs or alcohol where careers were threatened due to "unacceptable choices" that could be construed as a "bad reflection on the company". One could only assume that homosexuality was also on their list.

"I don't know, Glenn" I said. "This could make my situation worse."

"Na. If he gives you any shit, tell him to fuck off or you'll bust his beads all over the hall."

We made it to the church in time for the screening, Glenn laughing all the way. It was such a fun evening. So many people I knew and had come to care for. John, of course, as the writer/director, Glenn appearing as Divine in his role as Jacqueline Kennedy; Howard as JFK; David Lochary as the governess boyfriend; Bonnie (Mary Vivian Pearce) as one of the kidnapped models and many of our Marlborough group in the audience. Sweet.

******

We smoked weed and hashish back when a "nickel bag" meant five dollars' worth and was a goodly amount to share and relatively easy to come by. Two friends I won't name took a trip to Mexico where they purchased a small taxidermic alligator and stuffed its body with hashish. They packed it in a cardboard box and mailed it to themselves at their Baltimore address. Contrary to what one might expect today, it arrived safe and sound, the box never opened for inspection. If there were more serious drugs around, I never saw them nor were they ever offered to me.

A couple of acid trips took place in my presence. I was curious but hesitant. The media's chatter about "bad trips" included stories such as the one linking LSD to the suicide of Art Linkletter's daughter, though the accounts were ultimately proved to be false.

Oh, for heaven's sake" groused Glenn. "You've been around us when we're tripping and no one has jumped out of a window, have they?"

"We're were planning to take some on Friday night" said Van. "I've got an extra tab if you want it."

He knew I was intrigued and wavering.

"But if you are going to do it" he added "we should go shopping and find you a killer outfit."

At Hutzler's we found a sleeveless culotte dress with a rolled neckline in a knock off Pucci print in orange, black, lavender and white.

We paired it with sheer orange stockings and, lavender sandals-- a psychedelic outfit that set the stage for the evening.

By the time Friday evening rolled around and it was time to take the tab, I hesitated. I still wanted to have the experience, but the media stories continued to worry me even though I knew at least a dozen people who had done this and had a great time. I decided to err on the safe side by taking only half a tab. Van cut it for me on the ironing board in his kitchen; I swallowed it and waited for the show to begin. An hour passed without my noticing any of the expected color and movement nor any of the feared negative effects. I took the second half.

LSD changes the way you perceive the world, allowing you to engage with things as though you had new eyes. In some ways it is like being a small child again, with all the delight and appreciation for the world that one once experienced daily. An item that you see every day or think you "know" can take on new dimensions. People tend to get immersed in things - a flower, for instance - noting details such as the nearly invisible veins in a petal that they'd taken no notice of before. For an artist, it had the appeal of seeing things differently and newly.

We kept the rooms dimly lit. Colors seem more intense and lights appear to be brighter than usual. Often things or people appear to have a halo or aura. A person holding a lit cigarette will move their arm and leave a trail of light across your vision. Shapes can alternatively undulate and solidify. Candle flames dance to the music. When I closed my eyes, I saw a kaleidoscope of color and pattern. There was also an overall sense of well-being and contentment - one might even say euphoria – plus an increased sense of connectedness with the people I'd shared that evening with. Our "trip" lasted until Saturday's dawn at which time I went to my apartment to sleep, casually tossing my colorful outfit over a nearby chair before crawling into bed. When I woke several hours later, Singy was up and about. She pointed to my clothing draped over the chair and said, "I don't have to guess what you were doing last night."

I did acid a couple of times and had similar positive experiences. I remember only one small negative which for me demonstrated an individual's ability to remain in control on acid. On this occasion David Lehman prepared a spaghetti dinner for us and then we swallowed acid for dessert. As the evening progressed, people spread out to the various rooms of his apartment. A group of us were lounging about the living room listening to The Beatles Sergeant Pepper's album when the doorbell rang, and an unexpected visitor entered. He was a friend of David's, not someone we knew. I sensed a shift in the room, a vague paranoia. The man sat with David at a desk on the far side of the room. He was big and broad chested with dark hair and beard and he wore a red and black checkered lumberjack shirt. As I watched him, the black checks of his shirt began to slide about, blending with his beard and disfiguring his face.

"Nope" I told myself. "I'm not having that." I felt that despite the drug I still had the power to dictate my experience. The checks receded to his shirt almost immediately.

******

One of my evening painting classes was taught by Lila Katzen. To be honest, I wouldn't have chosen a class with her, but evening class options were often limited. While she could sometimes be insightful and supportive, she was strongly opinionated and had the reputation for being difficult and grumpy.

Lila gave us an end of semester assignment that she said would count towards a large portion of our grade. The instruction was to produce a work that was religious. Estranged from the religion of my childhood, I did not warm to the topic and I struggled to come up with an engaging idea. Ultimately, I decided to prepare three canvases, hinging them together to form a triptych, the three-paneled form used as altarpieces in the European Gothic period. Rather than focus on Christianity, however, I decided to use as my subject the symbols, designs and icons of the various eastern religions that I was learning about in my eastern art history class. In addition, I had also recently discovered the vibrant colors to be found in the small bottles of enamels manufactured for hobbyists. I was drawn to their beautiful jewel tones and hard high gloss finish that suited my subject matter well. Both the concept and the materials were far removed from my previous work, but I soon became wrapped up in the ever-evolving hard edge intricacies of the design. I painted temple columns adorned with mandalas and draped with vines, flowers and fruit. I added flamboyant birds, owls, snakes, fish, dragons, wheels if life, stele patterns and symbols, lotus flowers, poppies and bamboo.

As the painting progressed, Lila told me that she didn't like it.

She disliked it so much, in fact, that several weeks into the project she told me that if I persisted in completing it, she would not grade it. She followed that threat with a familiar tirade. "Paint" she said was "obsolete" and "archaic", a leftover from previous centuries, and we must justify our use of it in a world where many new and exciting media were being used.

I didn't agree and wanted to ask why she was teaching a class entitled "Painting" if she held that view. But I'd learned from observing the experiences of others that there was no point to challenging Lila when she was in one of her moods. I resented her threat about my work but doubted that she would follow through. Still, it would be a risk to continue. Tuition dollars were not to be squandered.

The next evening in 8C I began another project.

"Where's the painting you've been working on?" asked Glenn.

I told him about Lila's rant.

"You're doing a class with Katzen?" asked Van. "I've heard she can be a real bitch."

"You're not going to let her push you around are you?" asked Glenn.

"I think she's wrong" I answered. "But I don't want to fail the class."

"But you really liked the way your painting was going didn't you?" asked Glenn.

"Yes, it was going well but that's not the point."

"Finish it" he said firmly.

"Easy for you to say."

"You've got to stand up for yourself. She'll back down. She's a bully. She's trying to dominate you just like your mother. Aren't you sick of that shit?"

"And she can't fail you for using paint in a painting class" added Van. "You could take that to the dean."

"What's her work like?" asked Glenn.

"Very modern" I answered. "She does large installations constructed of Plexiglas and neon."

"Pffff. That's not modern. Neon's not new. Screw her" said Glenn.

"He's right." said Van. "Neon from the 1920's I think, and Plexiglas only a bit later. So she's not all that modern."

In the end I took their advice. Besides, I was really engaged with the painting and liked the way it was developing. I'd put so much into it and really didn't want to stop. And truthfully, at this late stage it would be hard to put in the number of hours needed on a new piece.

The next week, Lila announced that she had a show opening in New York and would be unable to attend our final class but had arranged for a friend to cover for her. Had she told her friend to refuse to grade my work I wondered, or had she forgotten all about her threat?

We were all quite surprised when the "friend" who came to class the following week was Grace Hartigan, the famous Abstract Expressionist. We were all familiar with her work and reputation. She told us that she had recently moved to Baltimore from New York and was just setting up her studio in the Fells Point area. As was usual, the class took turns presenting their projects to the group and Grace critiqued each piece. She thought my project was inventive, loved the images and color and gave me an "A" on the project. I danced back to the Marlborough. My whole group cheered when I told them.

"Katzen can hardly argue with Hartigan, can she?" Glenn asked. "And you can thank me now. I knew I was right."

In my notebook I recorded this quote:

"Painting is a job for a galley slave." – Gericault

And a poem rooted in art history:

Lila Katzen Lila Katzen
Oh, where will you be
When we usurp your power
Like Gericault from Dãvid?

******

Downtown Baltimore was a shopping mecca. There were five large department stores: Hutzler Brothers, Hoschild-Kohn, Stewart's, The Hecht-May Company and Braeger-Gutman. There were many others as well: Lane Bryant, Steiff Silver, Read's Drugstore, Hess Shoes, McCrory's 5 and 10, as well of dozens of small specialty shops. Shopping downtown was special to me as a child, and now that I was living downtown, it was an easy and tempting excursion.

One of my bargain purchases was a hat found on the sale table at Braeger-Gutman. It was a gray felt fedora, very Greta Garbo, and though I didn't habitually wear hats, it tempted me into impracticality with its style and sale price. Glenn was very taken with that hat; in fact, he liked it so much that he frequently snatched it from my apartment. We all knew Glenn had "sticky fingers"; he simply didn't see anything wrong with taking something if he wanted it. He would have made a good pickpocket because he was sly but also quite agile, so his actions often went undetected. It was hard to be angry with him, however, because he was also a very generous person. I was not, however, willing to give up my new hat. When I noticed that it had vanished, I had no doubt as to where it was and would set out to retrieve it.

"I've come for my hat."

"Hat, what hat? I have no idea what you are talking about."

I'd launch my search and always find it, taking it back to my apartment until the next occasion when we repeated the game. Eventually he lost interest in the hat at which point he presented me with a hatpin. It was not a stylistic a match for a grey felt fedora, but definitely a match for Glen's penchant for glitz. It is a weapon, over 4 inches long, the top of the pin studded with rhinestones.

"Every girl should have a hatpin, honey."

I thanked him, wondering when and with what I would ever wear it.

"I always carry a hatpin" he continued. "It is good protection. If someone gets fresh with you, you say stop and if they don't stop you stab them in the thigh with this. Or other places as need be."

I had no words and just smiled at him.

"You can smirk, honey", he said "but I'm telling you from experience, a girl can't be too careful!"

I still have that hatpin, along with other gifts he gave me: a rhinestone choker, a 3" pair of dangling rhinestone earrings, and my first "diamond" --actually a large teardrop chandelier crystal, an item that leads me inevitably to the story of the Hendler House.

******

Since first arriving at MICA, I had been enchanted by the stately homes that lined the streets of the surrounding neighborhood. They were of varying architectural styles including Georgian, Federal, Edwardian, Queen Anne and Gothic Revival. Most were three-storied and built of brick, stone and terra cotta. I was curious about their interiors and peeked discreetly through uncurtained windows, longing to examine the still existent detail and to envisage what it might have been like to live in such surroundings when they were in their prime.

Our street - Eutaw Place - was laid out and built in stages, starting in 1856. The street was 165 feet wide with a 72- foot central promenade, a swath of grass and flower beds containing curving walkways, statuary and fountains. Many architects think that the design was either a direct imitation of the Champ Elysee or built in rivalry to that Parisian promenade. The homes constructed on either side of the street were large and grand, most built in the late 19th or early 20th century.

From the 8th floor of the Marlborough we had a bird's eye view of the street, particularly the homes on the far side of the promenade. The house at 1710 was curious as it was always dark and there seemed to be no indications that it was inhabited. Some people said it was abandoned.

A quote from Greg:

"Somebody – I think it was George or Howard – brought up that old mansion across the street that had been unoccupied for many years. There was a story about the owners, a famous Baltimore family, I can't remember who. Anyway, the place was filled with amazing antiques. One room was all mirrors, ten feet high with a large onyx desk. I only went in once but remember seeing a line of guys coming out the front door with chairs, lamps, all kinds of antiques. They were all in single file, running across Eutaw Place and into the Marlborough."

I had been told by several people that the back door to the basement had been sitting open for some time, and that people from the neighborhood, including many from the Marlborough had removed various items from the house. One evening Van invited me to join him and a few others on a nighttime visit.

"Given how much you love old houses, you're gonna love this place" he said.

Van told me that the house had been the home of L. Manuel Hendler, the founder and owner of Baltimore's Hendler Ice Cream Company. I'd spent my childhood eating that brand of ice cream and was familiar with their kewpie doll logo and the tagline "The Velvet Kind" as well as the inventive and exotic flavors that they offered. Hendler's ice cream was considered premium and was served at fine hotels and restaurants. Baltimore's Southern Hotel served their tomato aspic ice cream as an accompaniment to selected entrees, and my Dad often purchased their eggnog flavor. As a child I never liked that flavor and later learned that it had been heavily doused with rum. The Hendler Company had, in fact, been required by the State of Maryland to maintain a liquor license in order to create a number of their flavors.

"Why is the house empty? I asked Van.

"Don't know. I was told that the older Hendlers died and that the place was being packed up, but the process stopped, maybe because someone contested the will. Everything seems to have come to a standstill. I don't know if that is true, but if so, I guess it never got settled."

Given the family's wealth it was also easy to see why people assumed that the contents of the house had been abandoned.

"They built a bigger house up on Lake Drive" said Glenn. "I think they took what they wanted when they moved there. They were probably just done with this place."

I wanted to accept Van's invitation for that nighttime visit but was hesitant. Our neighborhood was not considered particularly safe at night, but there was also the possibility that we would be caught. I could see the headlines, a final embarrassment for my parents "East Baltimore girl arrested for breaking and entering". But I went.

There were perhaps six of us that evening and we walked down the dark trash strewn alley behind the house. The yard was a jumble of long dead vegetation, a sagging fence, and heaps of debris and trash. The basement door was open as described, sagging inward to complete darkness. I already wanted to go back to the safety of the Marlborough.

Once we were inside, Van lit a candle to light our way. I soon learned that there were candles and matchbooks readily available at various locations through the house, indicating that visitors had been here multiple times. The flickering light of the candle revealed that the entry room had once been a kitchen, but it was now in rough condition and littered with trash and newspapers that had drifted in from the yard. Behind the kitchen was a larger dirt floored room that we supposed must have once held the building's mechanicals. There were some old pipes piled against one wall and pieces of what might have been the remains of a coal heating unit. In one corner a door opened into a wine closet, the racked empty bottles now coated with dust and cobwebs. On the north side of the room a flight of stairs led to the first floor. Here we found an assortment of crates and boxes which did give the impression that movers had been interrupted midway through their work. There were a several pieces of Victorian furniture as well as a scattering of lamps, pots, dishes and other household items. I wondered how many pieces of furniture had been removed by others in the neighborhood. I already knew that the silk upholstered Victorian settee and matching chair that sat before the fireplace in 8C had come from this home.

There were mirrored walls in what might have been the formal dining room. An adjoining room, perhaps a den or bar, was dominated by a large panel of stained glass featuring a plump male figure with beard and crown, joyfully holding aloof a mug of froth covered beer. I assumed that it must be King Gambrinus, the mythological northern European patron saint of beer and merriment, though I did wonder how he came to be in the home of a religious Jewish ice cream merchant.

In the front sitting room I noticed a curious item lying on a small table. It appeared to be a piece of white 20th century plastic set in a decorative mental frame. A rod projected from one side of the frame indicating that this peculiar item might have once been part of something larger. I picked it up and turned towards Van who stood nearby with his candle. My intention was to ask him if he knew what it was, but the item's identity was revealed in the light of his candle. It was a lithopane[vii], a panel of etched translucent porcelain. Lithopanes contain an image that appears in shades of gray much like a photograph, but it can only be seen when backlit by a light source. In this case it was an amazingly detailed image of a rustic farm scene and a young woman in 19th century dress balancing a large bundle of wheat on her head. Further research tells me that the projecting rod would have been set in a stand, allowing the framed image to be placed in front of a candle or lamp in order to display the decorative image.

My friends continued to poke about the house but with a candle in hand, I moved towards the front entrance. I'd been told that the walls of the entry hall were covered in worked leather and I wanted to see it. In passing the parlor I gasped when I saw my hazy candlelit image reflected in a tall, silvered pier mirror. I thought I'd seen a ghost.

The upper floor of the house contained additional empty crates, a spectacular marble bathroom, several bedrooms and an attic. Singy was particularly taken with the attic, where she found a trove of antique copies of Harper's Bazaar. A large family had once lived here and their things, once important to someone, seemed forlornly scattered about. I wondered once again what had happened. Change can come at you fast. Life slips through our fingers.

Several weeks later, Glenn solemnly presented me with a large teardrop crystal.

"Here, darling, a diamond for you."

He explained that it was part of a large and elaborate chandelier still gracing the second and much grander Hendler mansion just a few blocks away on Lake Drive.

"Well, that's another empty house now, honey, just like the one across the street. But, damn, I wanted that chandelier. I tried to pull that fucker out of the ceiling. I swung on it like Tarzan, but it wouldn't budge. A few of the crystals fell off and I brought this one for you."

I imagined him determinedly swinging from that chandelier and had no doubt he'd do it.

Hendler Chandelier Crystal and Divine Hat Pin

Divine Jewels

******

Several months later Glenn and George rented an apartment in the Emersonian Apartments on Lake Drive, near that same Hendler mansion where he'd swung from the chandelier. The Emersonian is another apartment building that once housed the wealthy elite of the city and has an interesting history. In 1895 Captain Isaac Emerson, the creator of the popular antacid Bromo-Seltzer, and known as the "Bromo-Seltzer King", built a large home for his family at 2500 Eutaw with a fine view of Druid Hill Park and Lake. In 1911 he and his wife divorced, and in the settlement she retained possession of their home. Captain Emerson remarried a short time later but apparently never got over the loss of his mansion. Since he owned the adjoining lot that stood between his lost home and the park, he set about building the eight story Emersonian Apartments in order to block his ex-wife's view. This story was noted in the Baltimore Sun[viii] where it was further noted that he "moved into one of the uppermost apartments so he would be looking down on her."

Glenn and George's new apartment was spacious with a large entry foyer, opening to the living area, its floor tiled in large alternating squares of black and white. There was a spacious kitchen, several bedrooms and a den. The den was chic with modern upholstered pieces and a stylish glass and chrome coffee table, strategically placed on a zebra skin rug. This was clearly the work of a designer. Van told me that Glenn had contracted with Jesse Benisch Interiors, an upscale interior design firm to decorate the entire apartment. The den was the first space to be completed but plans were for the balance of the apartment to be updated soon. Danger warnings flashed through my mind and with good reason. Glenn liked to live as though he were rich; I think he actually believed it at times and at others he simply chose to ignore reality. He'd made a number of large purchases in the past and his parents had bailed him out rather than see him prosecuted. I had no idea, of course, what Glenn and George's combined income was so perhaps it was okay. So far it seemed they were handling things, and Glenn was clearly delighted with his new home.

They hosted an extravagant New Year's Eve party with a champagne fountain bubbling in the foyer and platters of food arrayed on the kitchen counters. Van and I worked our way through the large crowd, most of whom we did not know. We spotted Paul and Howard across the room and went to great them. Paul pulled a Vicks inhaler from his pocket, pushed it towards me and said, "Smell this". That sniff was followed by a rush and mini explosion in my head. It caught me completely off guard and I could do little but watch Paul who stood there grinning widely. I learned later that the dispenser contained amyl nitrite, a prescription only vasodilator known on the street as "poppers". Amyl nitrite increases blood flow to tissues and is prescribed in response to a localized need, a fact I later learned when observing its use by an elderly family member suffering from angina. If I had known all that before I sniffed, I likely wouldn't have -- in any case, it wasn't a high I enjoyed.

Later, I was standing with Glenn when several young male party crashers reported to him their shock at seeing two men kissing in the den. "Yes, yes, I know" replied Glenn as he escorted them to the door "and there are a flock of fairies in the kitchen."

Glenn beamed through the entire evening. It was clear that he was enjoying his apartment and being the host of this rather extravagant party.

Several weeks later, when I dropped into 8C after work, I found Glenn, shirtless and wrapped toga-like in a blanket, wandering about the apartment. When he saw me, he dramatically placed the back of his hand against his forehead.

"Ah! Miss Melanie. Have you heard the news? I have lost Tara!"

I gave Van a questioning look.

"He's moved in with us" Van said. He got thrown out of his apartment. Apparently he overlooked paying the rent."

"Rhett, you are no gentleman!" shrieked Glenn. "But it is true. Tara is gone."

"What happened to all your stuff?" I asked.

"Ah, Miss Melanie, that horrid decorator woman came and took it away."

"Because he didn't pay for that either" drawled Van.

"Fiddle-dee-dee!" replied Glenn. "As God is my witness, they're not going to lick me. I'm going to live through this and when it's all over I'll never go hungry again!"

At that moment, the front door flew open and George entered

with a loud "Ta-Da", throwing open his ever present and too large raccoon coat to reveal the inner lining sewn with deep pockets, each one stuffed with a large brown jar.

"Oh, Spider!" said Glenn. "I feel much better now. You've got those lovely black beauties again."

I looked questioningly at Van again.

"Black beauties. Speed. Amphetamines. George works at a pharmaceutical company."

"Now I ask you, Miss Melanie" said Glenn "who in their right mind would let Spider near their drugs?"

"You do know that they are going to figure this out eventually, don't you George?" Van asked.

"Probably yes but no worries. I'll be gone by then. I'm going to quit before inventory" he replied.

"Are they dangerous?" I asked, remembering a news story I'd seen.

"Why would they be dangerous?" said Glenn. "All my clients take them. Doctors prescribe them to help all those chubby suburban housewives stick to their diets."

In truth, amphetamines were a widely used drug and had been available as an over the counter medication for years but were now available by prescription only. They were not viewed as dangerous at the time, and women flocked to "diet doctors" who regularly prescribed them as an anti-obesity medication. Always on a diet, that may have been the reason I first tried them. But I didn't need a doctor -- I had George -- who sold a mammoth jar for only five dollars. I kept them in the bathroom medicine cabinet for times when I needed to stay up late to complete an assignment or study for an exam. They never helped me lose an ounce. They did, however, attract a clientele. Singy and I were out one evening and came home to find four sad looking young men sitting on the floor of the hallway outside our apartment. They said they were friends of Vince's and that he'd told them about my supply because they were desperately looking for ways to fail their draft physicals the next morning. I didn't blame them. We were at the height of the Vietnam War and they were young and scared. I gave them the requested pills but afterwards decided to relocate my stash. They seemed innocent to me, but Singy was afraid I was going to get us arrested.

******

The next semester I enrolled in another evening painting class, this one taught by artist Dick Ireland. After several class sessions he announced guidelines for a final semester project, a painting to be completed outside of class time and which would account for a large part of our grade. The instruction was to complete a nude self-portrait, placing ourselves in an environment that represented our interests and defined us. The painting was to also make use of Renaissance perspective, a method that creates the illusion of great depth in a painting. Early and extreme examples from the Renaissance period might show the interior of a room with a view through a far window that that stretched over a faraway hill and into what unrealistically seemed to be the next county.

Over the following weeks I spent a lot of time on this project, shivering naked in my room, painting from my image in a full-length mirror. I posed in a standing position, holding a cluster of paint brushes in my left hand. Behind me an easel held a partially finished canvas, and the receding room contained a patterned rug, a table piled with books and art paraphernalia, a water pipe and a peace lily in a bright red pot. Through a distant window one could see the treetops and roofs of Eutaw Place disappearing into a grey fog. I was pleased with the result, and while a nude self-portrait was not something I felt comfortable showing around, Singy thought it was one of my best works.

As the semester drew to a close Mr. Ireland suggested that instead of everyone carrying their work to class, he would be willing to make studio visits. He suggested that if any of us lived near each other that we arrange to show our work together in order to reduce the number of stops he would have to make. Kit was also in this class and suggested that we show our work together and I agreed. As the date of the visit approached Kit asked if we could use his apartment for the visit as he was behind in his work and would probably be painting up until the last moment. That wasn't a problem for me and as events unfolded, I was quite grateful for his suggestion. Kit had a brawny build and his wiry hair and beard, as well as his often-serious expression, probably made him seem intimidating to those that did not know him. In fact, he was soft spoken, kind and more reserved than many in our group. At one point he had rather formally announced to us that he was gay, a disclosure that seemed uncomfortable for him though he seemed absolutely resolute in sharing his truth with us.

Mr. Ireland's visit to the Marlborough was scheduled for 6:00 PM though he didn't arrive until nearly 8:30. He was a gruff sort of fellow, and I didn't notice any difference in him that evening. My long day at work followed by no dinner and a two- and one-half-hour wait had rendered me quite grumpy myself. Kit said later that he'd though Ireland was a bit tipsy on arrival and he'd assumed that he'd been plied with alcohol as he worked his way through his previous stops. Ireland offered his not-quite-heartfelt apologies, tossed his jacket on Kit's couch and began the reviews.

He looked at Kit's painting first and made several comments and suggestions before moving on to mine. He studied my canvas for a long time and then said that he thought I hadn't done a particularly good job. The details of the room were interesting he said, and I had done a good job with the perspective, but he felt that the figure was not well executed and did not seem to be an accurate representation. I said that I thought that it was.

He shook his head. "One of two things seem to be the case - either you didn't actually work from life which was a central instruction of the assignment or you're simply not skilled enough to do an accurate representation."

He looked at the painting again, crossing his arms and cupping his chin in his hand. "But if you're interested in learning something from this critique, you could take off your clothes and pose next to the canvas so we can make an honest comparison."

I looked at him in disbelief and shook my head.

"That's fine. Your choice. You kids are always playacting at being cool and worldly but you're really prudish and provincial and, as it turns out, not all that committed to your work."

I glared at him. And then reached for the top button of my blouse.

"You don't have to do that Janet" said Kit.

"Of course she doesn't" said Ireland. "She can choose to use this to improve her work or she can continue to be an unprofessional little girl from East Baltimore."

"You don't have to do that, Janet" Kit hissed through his teeth.

But I did. Why? I wanted a chance at a fair grade, of course. But I can see in retrospect that while I fell for his trap, I wanted to prove to him -- but more so to myself -- that I wasn't the provincial little girl he accused me of being. I was also angry - angry that he said my work wasn't good enough, angry that he questioned my commitment, and the anger was not just for him but for the whole line of people before him that had told me in various ways that I wasn't good enough. Undressed, I stood next to the painting, grabbing a handful of Kit's brushes and assumed the same pose. Ireland was quiet and when he spoke it was not to address my artistic skills. His words were lewd, a discourse on how much he liked my body and what he'd like to do with it.

Kit flew off the couch, grabbed Ireland's coat, pushing it against his chest and propelling him out of the apartment into the hallway, shouting over his shoulder that I should put my clothes on.

"I better get a decent grade on this painting" I screamed as Ireland staggered down the hall "or I'll be meeting with the dean!"

Kit locked the door and plopped down on the couch. He was upset with me. "Why did you do that" he asked quietly. I didn't have a clear answer for him but despite the embarrassment, in a way I felt that I had won. Defiantly removing my clothes felt like giving the finger to Ireland as well as all the men I'd ever crossed paths with that didn't value women for our talent and brains, for what we can contribute and accomplish. I'd had enough of their shit to last a lifetime. It was anger and resentment, pure and simple.

******

It wasn't long before Glenn and George rented another apartment, this one at 159 Lanvale Street in a home built in 1874 by Joseph S. Hopkins, a nephew of Baltimore philanthropist Johns Hopkins. The building is most often known as the Mergenthaler mansion, as it was later the home of Ottmar Merganthaler, the inventor of the linotype machine which revolutionized the art of printing.

The front door opened to a tiled vestibule and then into an entry hall with tall double doors at either side. A curving staircase led to the upper floors but there was also a charming and somewhat shaky gilt elevator which would take us to Glenn and George's spacious third floor apartment. I was in the apartment several times but don't remember them living there for long. I don't know what precipitated their leaving, but assume it was money once again. They could, of course, have rented smaller or less luxurious units but Glenn simply could not. Such a suggestion would have him look at you as though you were mad.

Their landlady had apparently been forgiving to a point, mainly I suppose because they could be so damn likeable. But whatever the circumstance, this apparently well-read woman gave George a copy of this quote of Seneca when she finally turned them out:

"You need a change of soul rather than a change of climate. What pleasure is there in seeing new lands or in surveying cities and spots of interest? All your bustle is useless. Do you ask why such flight does not help you? It is because you flee along with yourself. You must lay aside the burden of the mind; until you do this, no place will satisfy you. That trouble, once removed, all change of scene will become pleasant. The person that you are matters more than the place to which you go."

George carried that folded and refolded sheet of paper in his breast pocket for weeks and spoke often of his resolve to refocus his life. He even moved home with his parents for a time. A group of us visited him in their perfect suburban home with a koi pond in the garden and George bunking in his childhood bedroom that resembled a ship's cabin. He didn't stay long.

******

The accidental meeting with Jim at the door of Leon's did not improve my situation at work as Glenn predicted. In fact, Jim seemed more intent on making my life miserable, and still there was no raise. A few weeks later and a full three minutes late, I found Jim lurking by the time clock once again.

"Ah, Miss Whittle. I see we are having trouble again today."

I didn't answer, but simply punched my timecard and headed down the hall to the library.

"It is amazing to me that you continue to have these difficulties, Miss Whittle" he said as he trailed after me down the hall. "I don't believe I've ever had an employee with such blatant disregard for our schedule."

"You never had any employees at all until you were moved from accounting" I muttered under my breath. I hung my coat and took a seat at my desk, gave him a bright smile and said that I'd be pleased to work through lunch if that would make him happy. He stood rigidly near my desk; his arms folded across his chest.

"As I told you before" he said with exasperation "that is not the point. It is my job to manage. Now, what about your monthly book orders? Will you have them done in time?"

"I always do" I responded, trying hard not to snap. In truth, I placed book orders weekly, sometimes more frequently, based on the needs of our staff and customers. His question showed how little he understood my job.

"Don't respond sharply to me" he said. "I am your manager, and it is my job to oversee." He leaned forward and tapped his pen on my desk for emphasis. "If an employee cannot do a simple thing like be on time each day, how can I count on that they're doing their job?"

I rose from my chair, speaking in a low but hardened voice. "Let me tell you what you can count on me for, Jim. You can count on my being a few minutes late a couple of times a month. You can also count on my working more than the required 40 hours per week. You can count on my doing a great job, a fact that is well established among the customers, engineers and salesmen that this library serves."

For a split-second I did consider adding Glenn's suggested taunt about "busting his beads all over the hallway" but I stopped myself, certain that that would be significantly over the top. I simply ended with a clear but firm request that he leave my office and let me do my work. He was shocked by that, I think, and he turned sharply towards the door and left. I knew that I might have put my job in danger, but I also felt empowered by my boldness in standing up to him. Smiling shakily I sank into my chair.

******

Changes I hadn't considered began to pile up quickly as the end of the school year approached. Singy would be graduating and moving home, and I could not afford to keep our apartment on my own. My friends who were fulltime students were going home for the summer, so none of them would need a Baltimore space until they returned in September. Van was among that group, and although he and I planned to share an apartment for the upcoming school year, I needed somewhere to live for the summer. George had recently rented a third-floor walkup on Park Avenue and said I could stay with him. I had no way to move my sparse furniture, so I essentially took only what I could carry. I made a series of trips from the Marlborough, my arms loaded with clothing, personal items and art supplies. I was unaware before moving that George's apartment lacked both air-conditioning and a refrigerator, so through that hot summer we were often not home and generally lived on inexpensive restaurant grub or junk food. I do not know where Glenn was at that time.

Van and I kept in touch through letters and occasional long distance calls. This was long before cell phones, and since I couldn't afford a landline we'd arrange by letter for a day and time for me to phone him in Florida. With a pile of quarters at the ready, I'd place an operator assisted person-to-person call from the coin operated phone booth outside the Park Avenue pharmacy. Below is a letter from Van addressed to George and me, though a bit of explanation is in order. We often made up rather silly pretend family relationships. At this time I was wife/mother, Van was husband/father and George and Steve were our "sons". I know, crazy. But if I didn't explain that this letter would be very confusing. Also, that summer I took a short trip to California to visit a friend who had left school to enter the Navy. The postcard Van mentions was from the Palace Hotel in San Francisco:

July 1968

Dear Wife & Son:

I am not having a good time in sunny Florida. I am having a lousy goddammed time and I am bored to death. I didn't get the job in Tallahassee because of the time involved. It's a special program and it runs to the 28th of September and that completely eliminated me. My education is far too important; my Mammy and Daddy said so. Besides, I had one hell of a time finding a place to live. The only place I could find with cathedral ceilings and a spiral staircase was 8 miles outside Tallahassee and I just couldn't see having to get up so early to go to work. Plus they had the crust to tell me to get a haircut. I told them I had just had it done. Such a shame because the Senators were stunning.

When I got home after I missed my fucking plane in Atlanta, I spent the week in Marianna and then went to Tampa to stay with my sister for a week. They have a stunning split level apartment with green shag carpet and a landscaped pool. Anyway, I looked for a job there but was unsuccessful. I went to several employment agencies but when I told them that it was just for the summer, they just kind of looked at me. Idiots. I guess they don't know who I am. The parttime or summer jobs didn't pay enough --$45 to $65 a week and I couldn't afford any of the apartments in town, so I had to come home. I went down to Panama City and they had nothing. I could sell insurance, but I don't have a car and I could be a mechanic but don't know the difference between the gas tank and the pistons, so I scratched that idea. I think I'll go to New York and hustle on 42nd street. I'd probably starve at that too.

I'm really upset about our youngest. I send him off to summer camp in Pennsylvania and he runs away to New York to live with the savages in that horrible beatnik place called the "Village". Seriously, is he still in New York? Father is very upset about this. Mother dear we have got to do something about this.

*By the way, Janet I got the postcard you sent me and I'm no longer worried about George. It's you. Anyway, that lobby my dear was **STUNNING!!!** The*

Crystal, Crystal, Crystal! Crystal! Let me pull myself together. I would have never left the Hotel (God I love a joint).

Oh well, you kids behave and write me again real soon, O.K.? Sorry I took so long in writing but I kept hoping I'd have some good news to tell ya. I miss ya'll so terrible much. It's much worse than I thought. Sometimes I catch myself calling your names but I forget there's a thousand miles separating us. Funny though, sometimes I think I hear ya'll calling mine.

Love, Stumpi

******

While I was certain that our group would stay in touch, I felt sadness over leaving the Marlborough. I feared we might lose the camaraderie and sense of belonging we'd shared while living in such proximity and wondered if we could maintain that magic in the outside world.

I'm not certain if there was a problem that had others leave the Marlborough but suspect there could have been some level of dissatisfaction, though I'd not had any issues with the building or management myself. Two years after our move, however, Baltimore City's Department of Housing and Community Development issued a vacating order citing a number of problems that were disputed by both management and existing tenants. Gerson Kroiz, the current manager, denounced the action as "an act of Naziizm" in the local newspapers, pointing out that many residents were seniors, working families or students from Johns Hopkins and MICA. The city seemed determined, and the Marlborough was ultimately condemned for building and fire code violations (such as those elegant 1907 open staircases). The building was subsequently renovated to supply senior housing under Section 236 of the National Housing Act. The work was done by Alan Greenfeld and Joel Zenitz, principles of Urban Development Company and Associates under contract with the city, two men who live in infamy for anyone who cares one iota about historic preservation.

A number of years ago I spoke with Bill Hazelhurst, the current owner of the Marlborough. Bill cares about the rich history of the building and expressed his distress at the damage that was done. "They must have gone through the building with bulldozers" he said, destroying nearly all of the original interior detail and "cutting the building into 288 terribly small units." It was, in essence, an ugly warehousing of the elderly. Bill did a second renovation in 1997, enlarging the units and getting rid of all but the largest efficiencies. He told me that during the renovation, he cut into the walls enclosing the staircases and removed the newel posts for display, the only surviving pieces he ever found of the Marlborough I remembered.

As September approached I rented an apartment for Van and me at 1602 Park Avenue, third floor front. Glenn was now sharing an apartment with Michael Gill just two blocks north. Other friends found places around Bolton Hill and several returned to the Marlborough. Our Park Avenue apartment became a milder version of 8C, with friends dropping by frequently but we were not all together as we once were, and I truly missed that. Everything seemed mellow, however, until Van and I received an eviction letter.

As it turned out, our landlord was in the process of upgrading an apartment on the second floor and had temporarily stored a roll of carpeting in the hallway. Our eviction was based on the accusation that the carpet "had been stolen by two of our friends" and the description given by another tenant left no doubt in my mind as to whom the culprits were. I stormed up the street to Glenn and Michael's. They were, of course, all batty-eyed innocence, shocked that I would accuse them of theft, but I stomped through their apartment and found the roll of carpeting stashed in the back bedroom. I was furious.

"Take it back" I said. "Or I'll call the police. I can't believe you did this! You didn't even need it. And you did it without any thought to the trouble you might be causing Van and I."

Docile and appearing contrite (they were just sorry to be caught) Glenn and Michael carried the carpeting back to our building. But there was no reprieve for Van and me; our landlord still wanted us to leave. He said he simply didn't trust our friends. In that moment neither did I.

My work schedule allowed little time for apartment hunting, so Van found a basement apartment on Read Street and arranged to have all our belongings moved. The apartment was further south and thus further from our friends. It was, however, convenient to Van's part time work-study assignment at Hutzler's department store and it also had a more direct bus route to IBM for me. It was also only two blocks away from the part time waitressing job I'd just taken at the Park Plaza. I'd never worked as a waitress unless you count the church suppers I served as a teenager. But given how tight my finances were, I was looking for additional income when Howard told me about the opening at the Park Plaza.

"Don't I need experience?" I asked.

"Probably. If they ask about experience, just tell them you worked down the ocean last summer. They'll never check it out."

I did as he said and was hired immediately. There was a uniform; a black mini dress with a frilled white apron that made me look like a French upstairs maid. The salary wasn't much but the tips were grand.

A Mount Vernon area landmark, the Plaza, which was built in 1842, had been a private home, a social club and several incarnations of restaurants. The front dining room was relatively sedate, and except for the long bar down the east side of the room, the space and menu might well qualify for a nice place to take Granny on her birthday. The large room north of the dining room housed Baltimore's first discotheque. As the evening grew later, the music got louder, the clientele younger and a retracting wall between the two rooms was opened to combine the space. As the restaurant became an extension of the disco, less food was ordered, but that was fine with me as I made much larger tips serving Brandy Alexanders, Screwdrivers, and Whiskey Sours.

An additional bar and restaurant called "The Schoolery" connected to our kitchen from the north side (the space now occupied by Khun Nine Thai and The Helmand for you Baltimore readers).

After last call, the Schoolery became a popular spot for breakfast. I was often scheduled to work that shift as well, serving platters of eggs, bacon and pancakes to the bar hoppers wanting to eat before returning home. I remember one night I had so much money that my apron pockets were stuffed. When I got back to the apartment, I surprised Van by tossing a considerable number of greenbacks into the air.

******

There was another Jim at IBM. I'll call him "Good Jim" to distinguish him from my nasty manager. "Good Jim" was a newly minted manager too, having been elevated to that position just a few months earlier. Previously he had held the position of porter, handling all the activities of our busy loading dock. Good Jim and I had known each other since I started working at IBM, but our interactions had increased significantly since my move to the library as he delivered to me the boxes of manuals I received from IBM's printing facility. Good Jim was a nice man, and we had a congenial, even friendly, but professional relationship. I didn't see him often after he moved to management as he now oversaw the shipping, receiving and parts division on the first floor.

One afternoon, as I was getting a cup of coffee from the machine in the break room, Good Jim entered. We greeted each other and chatted for a few minutes and when he asked the ubiquitous "How are you doing?" question, I found myself being more truthful than I'd been with anyone.

"I'm doing okay. Things are as good as they can be with Jim as my manager. Sometimes he is such a prick."

Good Jim laughed.

"Did you know he hired a guy as my assistant?" I asked.

He nodded.

"If I tell you what I think, can we keep it confidential?"

"You have my word."

"I just know he is paying him more than me. It is just not fair, especially since I never get an increase".

Good Jim raised his eyebrows and punched his order into the coffee machine.

"Didn't you get a raise when you moved to the library?"

"No. And all he will say when I ask is that my salary is 'within guidelines'."

Good Jim looked troubled, hesitated, and then bent down to retrieve his coffee.

"Do you know where my office is?" he asked.

"Sure."

"I'm going to go there now. You wait a few minutes and follow me. Quietly. Don't talk. Just come in quickly and close the door."

This sounded crazy, like a line from a television show like Mission Impossible or The Man from Uncle. But I liked and trusted Jim and so I followed his instructions. I stood in the break room for a few minutes, then tossed my coffee in the trash and headed down the back stairs. After I entered his office, he reached over and locked the door.

"I'm taking a big risk here." he said quietly.

He turned to his bookshelf and took down a binder, flipping through the pages to a section containing the salary scales for administrative employees. He ran his finger down the page until he found the entry for my position and softly said "I'm guessing you are not in this range?"

My eyes must have been wide. I shook my head no.

"You can never say where you got this information. I would lose my job."

Why did Good Jim take such a risk for me? Two reasons that I can see: firstly, he was a good and decent human being. Secondly, as an African American he had more than likely experienced the sort of injustice he saw in my current circumstance. I deeply appreciated his trust. This information fully confirmed my long-held suspicion that I was being treated unfairly. I carefully considered how I could use this information without putting Good Jim at any risk.

At first, I didn't share this information with anyone but eventually told Singy about it.

"He showed you the manual?"

"Yes. Even the low end of the range is more than what I'm being paid."

"What are you going to do?"

I sighed. "I don't think I can do anything locally without raising suspicion. And I can't mention salary ranges without having someone wonder how I'd know them. I knew it was wrong that I hadn't gotten an increase when I moved to the library. Now at least I know the truth."

"You have to do something" Singy said. "Ha! Maybe you should send Glenn down to straighten things out!"

I smiled, remembering Glenn and Jim's inauspicious meeting at the entrance to Leon's and imagining what a scene a second meeting might bring. Fortunately, I had already decided on a less risky plan.

IBM had an inhouse program called 'Speak Up'. Plastic wall bins containing forms for communicating with IBM headquarters in Armonk, New York were prominently displayed throughout the office. I'd been told that the original intent of the program was to solicit ideas and input from staff - particularly engineers - but I thought it might be a way to ask about my salary and hopefully have someone knowledgeable look into it. I wouldn't have to indicate what I knew about salary grades, but simply express my concern over not receiving increases even though my work was held in high esteem. I thought the company was decent, it was just my boss who wasn't. I picked up a form the next morning, worded my statement carefully and mailed it to Armonk.

Several weeks later I was at my desk working on a book order when I saw our district manager march purposively past my door on his way to the administrative offices. That in itself was strange, as we usually were advised of his visits well in advance and they were preceded by much hoopla. Could his visit had anything to do with the 'Speak Up' form I'd sent to Armonk? Surely not.

A half hour later Mr. Meador's secretary came to my door to summon me to his office. My stomach clenched. Maybe this really was about my query to Armonk. Had my actions helped me, or had I made a terrible mistake? My mother's warnings echoed in my head – don't bite the hand that feeds you; don't make waves, don't be ungrateful; know your place; be respectful; sometimes you have to pay the piper; disaster looms.

When I reached Mr. Meador's office, I found our district manager seated in one of the visitor chairs with Jim seated beside him and looking very uncomfortable indeed. Mr. Meador asked me to be seated and stated that the purpose of our meeting was to discuss my inquiry to Armonk.

There it was, out in the open. I took the indicated chair, my stomach tied in knots.

"Armonk was not happy" said the district manager. "Not happy at all."

He was a large, pudgy man, nearly bulging out of the visitor chair, his arms folded across his ample stomach. "And I'm not happy either" he added firmly, with a hard glare in Jim's direction "as it has completely disrupted my schedule and forced me to drive over from Washington, D.C. through morning rush hour in order to straighten this mess out."

I reminded myself to breathe.

He shifted in his chair, turning to face me. "It appears, Miss Whittle, that there have been several errors regarding your salary that have recently been discovered. While the sales and engineering staff hold your work in high regard, you were apparently not given some salary increases to which you were entitled."

I felt a sense of relief and celebration in the very real possibility of justice in his words but managed to keep hold of my professional decorum. And he was not done.

"Further study indicates that your move to the library should have resulted in a pay grade change and a salary increase that for some reason was never activated."

That sentence was accompanied by a withering glare directed at Jim who was now carefully studying his shoes.

"Please understand, Janet" said Mr. Meador. "This was just a paperwork error. It is certainly not company policy."

"A paperwork error on the local level" fumed the district manager, again glaring at Jim. "I regret that it wasn't caught in my office as it should have been, but we have now made it right."

He explained that my salary had been adjusted to its proper level and from now on my bi-weekly check would reflect the adjusted salary. In addition, I would be receiving an additional check that would represent the pay increase retroactive to the date of my move to the library as well as the regular performance increases I should have received.

"We hope", he continued "that you are willing to accept this solution along with our profound apologies that such mistakes were made and took so long to correct."

I nodded. I was speechless, intimidated by his position and assured tone but also delighted that the conversation had gone so well for me. I was also fully aware that Jim had done this on purpose. He had circumvented company guidelines, for which at least, he now seemed to be in a good bit of trouble.

I realized some years later that Jim's behavior had been a violation of the Equal Pay Act of 1963, a fact that IBM management was likely excruciatingly well aware. I expect that the person who read the Speak Up form that I'd sent to Armonk had seen the potential liability and contacted the district manager with instructions to clean it up. I don't know if my acceptance of their offer let the company off the hook for any legal claim I might have made, but truthfully, I didn't know my rights nor would not have known how to go about such a legal procedure at that time. I verbally agreed to the arrangement, delighted to have an increased income. The district manager rose from his chair, picked up his briefcase, nodded to Mr. Meador and gave one last long glare towards Jim before heading for the door. He stopped momentarily by my chair and said softly "listen, honey, if you ever have another problem, just pick up the phone. Call me collect. But please, don't write any more letters to Armonk".

I was overjoyed with the knowledge that I would soon be solvent and that my financial anxiety had come to an end.

"Good" said Glenn "now you can afford to go to dinner".

"Or maybe I could go back to school" I mused.

******

Over the next several weeks I gave that idea a lot of thought. What if I banked the retroactive salary check and continued to work both jobs? I would need enough money to cover both school and living expenses, but no matter how I worked the numbers, no matter how much frugality I was willing to endure, it was depressingly clear that I could not afford both. For the first time in two years I considered asking my parents if I could return home.

"Are you crazy?" said Glenn. "You'd be miserable."

"Don't" said Van. "You can't just leave. And yes, you'd be miserable at home."

I feared they were right, though my parent's coolness towards me had diminished somewhat over time. After I moved downtown, I'd been cut out of family events and holidays, but the relationship with my parents had slowly softened, and I thought that my Dad had likely been responsible for that shift. I'd visited them several times; once Van went with me and we'd been invited to stay for dinner. When we left that evening, my mother, not knowing that we were roommates, gave us each a bag of the apples they'd purchased at a local orchard. As we stepped out on the porch, Van leaned over and laughingly whispered in my ear "So what are we going to do with all these fucking apples?"

Before Van and I moved in together, I was cautioned against it by our friend Celeste. "Sharing an apartment with a guy who is not your lover is not a good idea" she said. "I know women who thought they could do that and then one or the other of them couldn't handle it and it became a real source of heartache."

That seemed silly. Van and I were good friends, and I couldn't in my wildest dreams imagine such a scenario.

I continued to grapple with the financial realities of a possible return to school. Could I come up with an adequate sum if I waited another year or would it take longer?

"Both terrible ideas" said Van. "You need to tie down some financial aid or a scholarship in order to make it work. Make an appointment with John Sutton and see if he can help you. Tell him you're a friend of mine."

John Sutton was the dean of students and while I'd not had much interaction with him, I knew that he was generally held in high regard by the students. With Van's recommendation, I booked the appointment. John encouraged my idea of my returning to school and while there was little aid available for the upcoming semester, he offered advice on future sources of funding. He then asked about my relationship with Van and seemed surprised that we were friends and not lovers. He said that he had just assumed that ours was the usual "shacking up" relationship he often saw among students and asked why I thought we hadn't taken that route. I said that I had assumed that Van was gay, and in any case, our friendship would not be worth risking. Sutton asked if I didn't think that we were perhaps doing each other harm by living together and told me that he'd seen other similar relationships result in pain and in some cases there were severe emotional repercussions. The conversation frightened me. Were Van and I headed for something painful that we couldn't see? I was also vaguely suspicious that the conversation had veered so far from the original topic. It almost seemed planned. Had Van said something to Sutton that brought on this inquiry? Sutton suggested that I consider taking some action before either of us was hurt. I left his office knowing that I needed to talk with Van.

Van and I had a complicated relationship. We were never lovers but good friends who respected and cared for each other. But now that we were spending so much time together, I found myself becoming more attached. It set off mild alarm bells for me, and also a remembrance of Celeste's warning but now John Sutton's questions brought the possible dangers to the forefront of my mind. In the past, I'd never even remotely considered a more intimate relationship, but somehow living together seemed to have shifted our balance. We talked about it. It was a hard conversation.

Van said that before we'd become roommates, he'd seen the possible hazards of living together but thought it was something we could handle. He said that as time passed, he'd thought about a more intimate relationship and considered making a sexual advance but hadn't acted on it because he wasn't sure how I would react and didn't want to take the chance of damaging our friendship. It was strange to learn that I wasn't alone in these feelings, but I was also glad that we had never followed up on it. I, too, feared we'd do harm to a relationship that was very special to me. He was one of my biggest supporters, and I loved him for the person that he was.

My confusion over Van's sexual leanings seemed to complicate the situation further. I'd assumed he was gay because so many of his friends were, and stereotypically, because he was a fashion major and loved a lot of glitz. But he'd spoken many times of a girl named Donna back in his hometown in Florida. He'd apparently been in love with her and was devastated when she broke up with him. He also commented often on the attractiveness of women at work. Was he bisexual? I suppose I could now assume so, although in my naivety at that time it wasn't a term I'd heard or understood.

We talked for hours as we often did, but I could see that there were but three options: We could move to a more intimate relationship, one that I knew at a gut level might bring one or both of us sorrow. Or we could continue living together in a situation that now felt awkward, pretending that things hadn't uncomfortably shifted and that we were still how we used to be. Or I could leave. Moving home with my parents now seemed a more pressing option for my future. Van didn't want me to leave but he was as supportive as he always had been.

I spoke to my parents and they agreed that I could return, surprisingly not voicing any restrictions. It was, however, an extremely hard decision. I loved my parents - that was never the issue. The challenge was that they were in their fifties with standards and world views formed in the 1920's, while I was twenty-one with an entirely different viewpoint in a world much changed and changing faster. Our generational gap seemed wide. While my father had always been far more the most mellow and accessible, I now could only hope that that my mother's previous unbending views had softened. I had definitely become stronger and more certain of my course, more self-confident and less inclined to be managed.

I continued working at IBM, intending to give several weeks' notice at the end of the summer. I also continued my Park Plaza waitressing job, though my parents didn't like it. The tips were too rich to forfeit and I hoped to continue working there through the school year, so that I'd have spending money. I narrowed my focus to saving as much money as I could, successfully completing my application to MICA, and preparing for what felt like a deep academic dive. Cerebral shifts were required. I wrote in my journal: "Even disregarding the money involved, it is my mental state that must be adjusted. I've gotten lazy. It has been so easy to just have a good time for the past two years, so I have to get everything in perspective. I have to keep school first in my mind, holding tight and not letting go. If I don't give it my best now, I might not get another chance."

While there were some adjustments to be made as a result of my move back home I now found it easier to avoid dissention. My mother tried in small ways to manage me, but I generally avoided it. I noted in my journal that in some ways I had to "resolve to pay with my freedom in order to achieve my goals."

No matter how much I loved my downtown friends and missed the fun-loving lifestyle I'd enjoyed with them, I also felt the need to put some space between us. Schoolwork had to come first. And given the disorienting and muddled turn our relationship had taken, this was especially true of my friendship with Van.

There were a few times that I saw everyone. The first was a New Year's Eve party at Barry's. Barry lived in the Marlborough, though he wasn't part of our usual crowd. He was a friend of several other friends, including David with whom he shared a love of opera. I knew about the party and several friends called to ask if I would be there. I was tempted. Fun was in short supply in East Baltimore. Van called several times encouraging me to attend. At one point I had decided to skip it and yet when he kept calling, I weakened. It wasn't just that he could be charming and persuasive, but that I really missed the friends and life I'd left behind. Barry did things classy, as I'd expect. Drinks, hor d'oeuvres, weed, lots of people I liked. It was lovely to see everyone. The evening felt bittersweet.

There was music and dancing, and Van pulled me to the dance floor. The stereo played one of his favorites, "The Supremes Sing Rogers and Hart", the cut was "My Romance", and he held me close, singing the words near my ear.

My romance doesn't have to have a moon in the sky

My romance doesn't need a blue lagoon standing by

No month of May, no twinkling stars

No hide away, no soft guitars

My romance doesn't need a castle rising in Spain

Nor a dance to a constantly surprising refrain

Wide awake I can make my most fantastic dreams come true

My romance doesn't need a thing but you

My romance doesn't need a thing but you

I was confused and not in a good way. What was he doing? Had he forgotten or misunderstood our past conversation? Surely not. And because he was a kind person, I knew he would not do something to purposely hurt me. What was happening? It was, I think, an example of a type of man-think that I've experienced a number of times since then: the assumption that something once discussed was now flat and totally handled, a point not as easily reached by the female mind. I couldn't do this. I needed more time away.

On another occasion I attended a party that Glenn gave at the new Sheraton Hotel downtown. Once again, it was great to see this group of much loved people. Glenn adored a party, and he was an excited and fluttering host. He'd arranged for a private dining room with sliding doors to a terrace. There were floral arrangements, food, alcohol and weed, the room so thick with the smell of it that the waiters must have gotten high just from walking in and out of the room. Many years later, I learned from Glenn's mother's book "My Son Divine" how often she and her husband had had to cover Glenn's expenditures. One instance she mentioned was their having to cover a bad check he'd written for alcohol purchased at a local liquor store for a party he gave at the Sheraton Hotel. I expect it was the one I attended.

I did feel a bit like a square stodgy fossil that evening as I imagined the narcs that might soon dash through the door. It was one thing to smoke weed in the relative safety of 8C, quite another to do so in such a public place. Jail was not what I needed at this point in my life. I left the party earlier than planned, feeling that disharmony but also the pull of schoolwork that must be completed. Sadly, I also felt a vague estrangement, as if this were not my world anymore. In truth, I had felt our worlds imperceptibly drifting apart ever since leaving the Marlborough, that magical time when we were all in the same building. But we were all now moving in different directions.

******

My three night a week waitressing job at the Plaza brought me downtown for work and explains how I came to be there – and thus stranded -- on the evening of April 6, 1968, the night of the Baltimore riots.

Despite the fact that only two days had passed since the assassination of Dr. Martin Luther King, it was a usual night at the

Park Plaza. Our clientele was all white and mostly suburban; the disco was crowded, the music loud, the strobe lights flashing.

I went to the kitchen to place an occasional food order and found Gloria, our young African American cook, hovering near a small radio. "There's trouble brewing" she told me. "Some kids broke a window and looted a store."

Gloria was probably the only person in the building who was aware of what was going on in the outside world. Each time I returned to the kitchen she updated me on the latest news report -- more windows smashed, additional stores looted, a large furniture store going up in flames. In those days before cell phones, in the windowless strobe-lit room roaring with the Motown beat of Aretha Franklin and Smokey Robinson, the remaining staff and certainly the customers were completely unaware. I shared my concern with my fellow employees. The bouncer and his wife smiled benignly and showed me a small pistol tucked in a blue bedroom slipper behind her hat-check counter. One of the bartenders asked me to step behind the bar where he showed me a sawed-off shotgun hidden on a deep shelf behind the bar's ice well.

"Nothing to worry about" said our manager, Mr. Krumm "the police will soon have things under control."

My next trip to the kitchen found Gloria more upset. The news reports indicated that the chaos had widened. A growing number of businesses had been looted and ransacked, there were more fires, including a 4-alarm blaze now consuming a large grocery store. Young men were attacking police with rocks and bottles. The mayor, with his police department nearly overrun, had asked Governor Spiro T. Agnew to send in the National Guard. An 11PM to 6 AM curfew had just been announced.

"I've got to get home to my kids" Gloria wailed. "The buses are going to stop running!"

"You should go" I told her. "It's okay, really. Krumm won't even notice. He's going to have his hands full, and he's going to have to announce the curfew so that everyone else can get home too."

I left in search of my coworkers. The disco was still going full beat, the strobe lights bouncing across the dance floor, the music loud. The disparity between that room and the news from the outside world was nearly incomprehensible. The staff was now taking the situation seriously and we circled Mr. Krumm in the lobby. He remained resolute in his plan to stay open, no doubt fearing the halt to his ringing cash registers. "You have to tell people what is going on" we insisted. Finally after some argument - particularly the specter of his possible liability -- he relented. The house lights were turned up, an announcement was made, and customers poured from the building.

I stood on the front steps of the Plaza. Mount Vernon was empty and eerily quiet. I looked east down Madison Street, the route of my bus home and could see fires burning in the distance. I knew it was unlikely that I could return to my parent's home that evening. One of our service bartenders who lived several blocks away offered those of us who were stranded a roof for the night. His very pregnant wife graciously welcomed us. We piled into a single car and drove the short distance, detouring to pass the Fifth Regiment Armory, an imposing fortress-like structure built in 1901. Along the streets surrounding the Armory were row upon row of open military transport trucks, their benches filled with grim-faced National Guard troops, all holding bayoneted rifles. It seemed the world had gone mad.

Greg wrote about this time at the Marlborough:

"One place I felt safe was on the roof. I loved it up there. When Martin Luther King was assassinated we had martial law curfews. I remember you could do a 360 degree turn up on the roof and see fires all around the city. We watched the looters smash windows in stores. One day we watched them rob the A&P. They would bring out stuff and stash it in a construction site across the street. Bob, Lee and I snuck down when the looters went back for more and we took their stash. Stealing from the looters.   Eventually I remember national guardsmen on every corner, heavily armed. One day a tank went by on Eutaw Place. This was one wild time, and the old Marlborough was our fortress."

*****

My return to school was joyous, an absolute deep dive. Over the next two years I took painting classes with a variety of instructors, several life drawing and advanced drawing classes, photography, and two semesters of advanced color taught by Reba Stewart, who'd been a student of the famed Josef Albers at Yale. There were various seminars and independent projects and lots of reading. Our academics included Man as Spirit, an inquiry into spirituality led by an Episcopalian minister, a Catholic priest and Jewish rabbi; scientific readings, "History of Modern Art, and "History of Primitive Art" taught by Lenora Foerstel who had spent years in New Guinea with anthropologist Margaret Mead. Alan Ginsberg read us poetry from the clock tower of the old B & O station as we lounged stoned on the grassy lawn. I made the Dean's List. I had returned to being the student I had been before Marty.

One evening my father commented on an article in the Baltimore Sun about some "crazy kids" who had been arrested for indecent exposure on the Johns Hopkins University campus. He folded the newspaper and began to read aloud. I realized instantly that the article was about my friends -- it was John Waters and his Dreamlanders who had run afoul of the police. They had been filming a fairly innocent scene for John's new film, Mondo Trasho in which Divine fantasizes the nudity of a hitchhiker played by Mark Isherwood. During the filming, the group was spotted by a University security guard who thought that they were making a porn film and called the police. John has related this story in the past with this funny punch line: "The cops raided the set and they busted all of us, but not Divine. He got away. And he was in a red 1959 Cadillac Eldorado convertible with the top down and a gold lame toreador outfit with a nude man in the car – in November. And they couldn't catch him."[ix]

Divine in John Water's Film Mondo Trasho, 1969,
Copyright Dreamland Productions.

I still saw some of my old Marlborough crowd, at least four of whom were in my graduating class. We sometimes saw the others from our group who remained in town. George would show up at my parent's home, all polite and proper to whisk me away in his convertible. My mother thought he was my boyfriend. We went out to dinner or to the movies, once splurging on live theatre tickets to see Celeste Holm star in "Auntie Mame" at the Morris A. Mechanic Theatre. On one occasion we went to the Baltimore Yacht Club where his parents were members. We drank pink lady cocktails in the bar and then hung out on his parent's boat smoking hash. When it was time to leave, we felt so unsteady that we were afraid to walk the gangplank to the dock. Giggling, we crawled across to avoid falling into the river. Chuck took me on several outings on his motorcycle, adventures I am grateful to have survived since he told me years later that he had been very high on a mixture of things. John, Divine, George and the balance of the Dreamlanders moved to Provincetown, Chuck moved temporarily to suburbia, David Lehman bought a $1 city owned house on Lake Drive. When he moved from the Marlborough, he took the beautifully carved fireplace mantel from his living room and installed it in his new home. Kit left for California, gifting me with one of his paintings. On the back in bright inks he wrote:

In the Marlborough

May 22 Day 1969
Baltimore, Md 21217

Dear Janet,

The Day is Blue sky

Sunshine day – atop

The OLD MARLBOROUGH

And I'm to fly away

Some day to GREEN

SUMMER DAYS – AND

Divine Intervention

I will remember those

Days I knew you

Dear Janet —

Love, Kit

Van began a relationship with Peter. After graduation they moved to New York where Van had taken a position as an illustrator at Women's Wear Daily. About once a month, telling my mother that school assignments required my visiting New York museums and galleries, I would take the train to Manhattan and spend several days with them. They had a loft near the Port Authority, and in the morning when they went off to work, I would head uptown to immerse myself in galleries and museums. Our evenings were full of activities, dinners out, strolls through the Village, parties, shopping, dancing in Central Park. Van later became the makeup artist for John's films and was the creator of Divine's unique and high camp look including his partially shaved head that made room for those outrageously arched eyebrows.

I met my future husband in photography class in my senior year. While my mother ultimately became truly fond of him, in the beginning she disapproved. He was older than I, she argued, and of a different religious background. Her opinion did not improve when I told her he was divorced. When Irv and I decided to marry, we opted for a small ceremony in the courthouse chapel, deciding to spend our money on a six-week honeymoon in Europe instead.

"If you aren't going to have a big church wedding and invite my family, I won't be there" my mother told me. Divine's unending admonishments to not let myself be bullied echoed loudly in my brain.

"We'll miss you" I said.

I'm certain that my father intervened once again because my parents did attend our wedding. Bonnie Boom-Boom was our maid of honor. When we returned from our European adventures, Irv and I relocated to West Virginia where he was a partner in a thriving real estate business. I continued to paint, did some graduate work at MICA, dabbled in writing, and indulged my hippie gene by planting an organic garden. Many of our friends were business associates of Irv's and in a likely overzealous intention to protect his position in this relatively conservative community, I didn't speak in any detail of my former life in downtown Baltimore. Irv and I would often laugh over the fact that the president of a local bank that provided significant financing to his company, expressed great relief that Irv had "married and settled down", never knowing that I was surely the wilder of the pair. We traveled, returning to Europe on several additional trips. We spent gourmet weekends in DC with friends, staying at the Hay-Adams Hotel across from the White House and enjoying wonderful dinners at iconic restaurants such as San Souci, Rive Gauche and L'Escargot.

One late Saturday evening after one of those dinners, we drove through Georgetown searching for a place to buy early editions of Sunday's Washington Post before heading back to the hotel. On M

Street we saw a large crowd queuing up at the movie theatre where the flashing marquee announcing the newly released film Pink Flamingos. I sat in the back seat of our friend's black Cadillac with a secret smile on my face, excited for and proud of my old Marlborough friends and thinking of the old me, the East Baltimore one and the Marlborough one, both of whom now seemed so far away.

******

I have often wondered about the people who influenced me negatively in my youth. What was their purpose? I read of similar behavior online almost daily and wonder if it is now even more commonplace or perhaps just more visible as a result of social media. Are people intentionally mean or simply thoughtless? Do they obtain some level of enjoyment or sense of safety from their attempts to make others feel small or do they simply not notice the extent of the hurt they cause? Are they grappling daily with their own hurts or fears, fending off their own sense of inadequacy and failure by attacking others? I suspect that is so.

We humans are so fragile. We carry with us internal lists of what is wrong with us – our failures, weaknesses, our terrible faults - compiled from the comments of others and our own cruel self-assessments. We live with the ever-present possibility that our flawed self will be publicly identified and that others will see and recognize all the faults and weaknesses we are certain that we have. Some of us hide ourselves away to varying degrees as I did. Some build images that they project into the world, patterning themselves on some dreamed of perfect self instead of joyfully being who they are. Others display their sense of insufficiency by finding fault with or attacking others, creating a comparison that allows them to feel better about themselves and the internal criticisms they also live with daily. Ultimately then, most of us are afraid but express it differently, cloaking our compassion, our humanity, our basic good heartedness out of fear of being found a fraud.

When I was young and people told me that I wasn't good enough, smart enough, strong enough or pretty enough, I believed them. I believed them for too long. And while I didn't have what I needed and longed for from so many, I found it in my group of downtown friends.

I realize that my complaints about my childhood are microscopic compared to the atrocities that many children experience on this earth. I fully recognize that my circumstances were far, far better than so many. Still, I am glad that I generated the will to resist the rules of my parents and the limited future they saw for me, a path not horrible but clearly not a fulfillment of me. I am grateful that as small as I felt, I was courageous enough to leave that environment and venture out into the world. I am grateful to Dr. Theresa Thompson, my high school guidance counselor, for opening a door to a different future with that initial scholarship. I am grateful that I fought for my education against some odds and despite my mistakes. Realizing that I could have a different future made me stand up for myself, and in the end I discovered that I was brave, not in the grandiose way I had imagined but in some steadfast, dug in and stubborn way I had managed to be true to myself and to head out on a path I wanted.

I am grateful for my downtown friends – people I would have been unlikely to meet on the streets of East Baltimore. They were a huge contribution to the growth and learning I needed, and they provided me with friendship and support at a fragile but expansive point in my life. I'd been lucky to find people who encouraged me, championed me and empowered me. They helped me gain a confidence and strength I am not certain I would have fully realized without them. While these friends enriched my life in various ways, it was Divine, Singy and Van who became my trusted triad of support, pushing me out of my comfort zones and towards new experiences and views, urging me to consider fresh interpretations of who I was and what my future could hold.

So many of the people in my memories are gone from this earth. My father died in 1999. My mother mellowed over the years, accepting a long list of changes in her family and the world that softened her behavior and world view. After my dad's passing, Irv and I moved her in with us for eight years before her health dictated a move to a healthcare environment. I oversaw her move from my childhood home into ours, then to the small apartment at the healthcare facility and again to the skilled nursing section where she ultimately left this earth at age one-hundred and one, all the while trimming back the seemingly endless possessions, all the dented furniture, saved papers and ragged pieces of embroidery, until at last we were left with scarcely enough to fill two boxes. All those worldly things that were so important to her, gone. Observing her tendency to save everything and then her true anguish as she let things go piece by piece, taught me yet another valuable lesson. As a result I've learned to more easily let go of accumulated belongings. They really aren't the stuff of life; people and memories are. That knowledge and the resulting freedom were of great value and underlined an oft repeated maxim of my paternal grandmother: "There are no pockets in a shroud.".

My mother's mind was sharp until the end, though she sometimes attempted a rewrite of history. I overheard several conversations when she told others that she had always wanted to go to college but that her family could not afford it. That, she said, was why she had "worked hard to assure that both of her children obtained a college education". I did not dispute her comments; after so many years, all I could do was be amused.

Many of my downtown friends are gone: Singy Tevis, Divine, Van Smith, David Lochary, Howard Gruber, Kit Throssell, George Tamsitt, David Lehman, Bob McCormack and perhaps more. When Divine died in 1988 he was only 42 years old. Like so many, I was shocked and deeply saddened. Divine was entering a new phase of his career and was scheduled to begin a recurring role on FOX's "Married with Children". He had certainly solidified the stardom he dreamed of those many years ago.

At the time of his death, Irv and I were living in Florida and struggling with some financial and life issues that made it impossible for me to travel to Baltimore for the funeral. I read the many articles in the media including The New York Times, The Village Voice, The New Yorker and People Magazine. Divine's mother, Frances Milstead wrote that she couldn't remember all of the famous people she met at the funeral but mentioned Katey Sagal, Ricki Lake, Jerry Stiller and Anne Meara in her book. David Lehman wrote to me, describing the funeral home and the deep sadness of all our old friends:

"Went to see Divi laid out. Pat Moran was grieving; every time someone else came in she broke down all over again. John was just about keeping himself together. Howard looked great and Barry kept asking him 'How is your health, I mean how are you?' Howard just said 'Fine, fine!' Lots and lots of flowers. One from Whoopi Goldberg said, 'See what a good review can do to you". A film company which Glenn was signed to do a TV sitcom for wrote 'If you didn't want to do this show, why didn't you say so?' I missed Van and George. Saw Steve, Mink Stole and Mary Vivian Pearce. I didn't go to the funeral or wake; 300 people showed up and Towson traffic was backed up 45 minutes".

After returning to Baltimore several years later I made a point to visit Divine's grave and have done so a number of times. Prospect Cemetery is small and peaceful and sits on a hill very near where Divine once worked at the James Hair Salon. It is apparently a place of homage for many as his stone is marked with messages in lipstick and there are always flowers and small mementos.

Singy, our bundle of energy, died in 2002 as a result of complications following a delicate heart surgery. The doctors told her that her condition stemmed from a congenital defect that apparently had grown worse with age. She had been advised that the surgery was risky, but she was resolved to take the chance as it was hard to breathe and she felt constantly exhausted and worn. I was with her, her brother and her medical advocate when she was removed from life support, her loss another wound to my soul.

When Van Smith died after suffering a heart attack in 2006 I was again devastated. He had been living in his hometown of Marianna, Florida and was buried there. At a later date, John Waters arranged a private memorial service that was held at the American Visionary Art Museum in Baltimore. I saw people there that I hadn't seen in years, all drawn together to both celebrate and mourn a man that we all thought the world of.

Irv and I have been married for 50 years and he is my best friend. Together we have experienced much joy and weathered some of the harsh and scary events of life. We have two magnificent and deeply loved children. I'm sure I made any number of mistakes as a mother, but I tried my best to not push them to fit some design of mine, feeling that my responsibility was to protect them while they grew into the people they wanted to be.

I've continued to paint and write. I've not followed a career path but have done a hodge-podge of things including working at a low-income food coop, insurance sales, owning and managing an award-winning restaurant, and several administrative positions at Johns Hopkins University. In 1999 I earned a master's degree there.

Many have survived from that group/time that I know of: John Waters, Chuck, Bonnie Boom-Boom, Bonnie Pearce, Mink Stole, Pat Moran, Vince Peranio, Steve, Lee Hoffman, Greg, and Debbie. There are others we have lost track of. I hear from several of these friends online and through occasional notes and Christmas cards. I always enjoy John's holiday cards which are creative and fun. Until I moved from Baltimore last year, I would see both he and Vince at various art events in the city. I have been impressed by the fact that despite his career and fame, John always warmly greets those of us he remembers from our long ago past. He might not like my saying it, but truthfully, he is a gentleman. Chuck, Susan, and Pat are still in Baltimore as well. So to those gone and to all still here, thank you. You were a gift at the perfect time.

5 Addendum – letters and pictures

This map shows the original floor plan of the Marlborough's first floor.

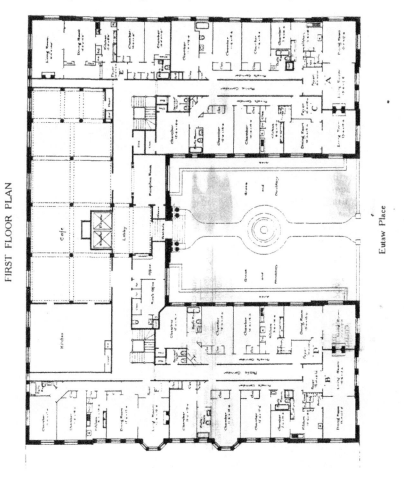

FIRST FLOOR PLAN

This map shows the original design of all additional floors. I have indicated the location of 8c and 8j; note that they were once one large apartment.

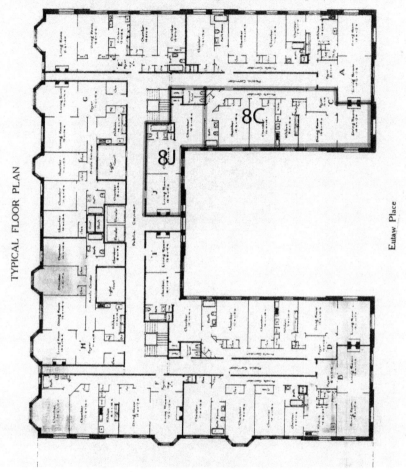

TYPICAL FLOOR PLAN

Eutaw Place

Van's High School Photograph

artist: Van Smith
representative: Evelyne Johnson
(212) 532-0928

Van's Business Card
New York City

George and I pose for photos at the direction of
Bonnie Boom Boom

IT WAS EASTER WEEKEND AND MANY WERE AWAY OR WITH THEIR FAMILIES. VAN, STEVE AND I WERE STILL IN THE MARLBOROUGH AND OUT OF CIGARETTES. WE WENT OUT TO BUY SOME, ONLY TO FIND THAT ALL THE BUSINESSES WE APPROACHED WERE CLOSED FOR THE HOLIDAY. REASONING THAT THE TRAIN STATION WOULD STILL BE OPERATIONAL, WE HIKED OVER TO PENNSYLVANIA STATION, WHERE WE WERE ABLE TO PURCHASE CIGARETTES FROM A MACHINE. THERE WAS A PHOTO BOOTH NEARBY, SO WE INDULGED IN A PHOTO SESSION.

Divine Intervention

Van had a problem with his back. I don't believe I ever heard the exact diagnosis but had the impression that it was a form of congenital scoliosis. While at home in Florida during the summer he had a surgery, and this letter mentions that experience.

Dear Janet,

Got your letter and what the hell am I going to be surprised about? Are you behaving yourself? I mean you have been know to flip-out on a few occasions as I re-call. By the way are you still seeing Jerry? I see you avoided the subject in your letter, or did you? Oh well enough of that, I will tell you my problems. After all this aggrevation I have gone through I still have to go for a pre-induction physical because they want to check me themselves. I'm taking at least a thousands letters from my doctors to prove my conditions and I'm also going to take doctor Scotts just in case the others don't work. I pray I don't have to use it because if I do there are going to be some hard times ahead.

I got a delightful card from Chuck the other day and it couldn't have come at a better time because I had just found out about my physical and I was extremely depresate and his card

picked me right up again and had
me smiling all day. I love ole'
chuck so much. I love all of ya'll
so much and you can't begin to
believe how much I miss ya'll.
If everything goes alright I'll be
in Baltimore between the 18th & 23rd of
July, I wish to hell I knew the
exact date.

    Speaking of Baltimore how
is that gorgeous place. Marianna
stinks, the monsoons have set
in so its really lovely here.
Sun-shine state my ass!!!!!
Haven't seen sun for days.
Honey! you should see the "gash"
that butcher planted on me; if
it's an inch its 30". Frankly I
think he got just a little carried
away, but I've decided to have
plastic surgery like Elizabeth
Taylor, for after all, I'm a star
too! Say "hi" or "fuck you" or
whatever ya'll are saying
these days to everyone for me.
Write me back ok?

            love
          Stumpé

<u>Letter from Steve</u>

Aug 29 1969

Dear Janet ★

Hi!

Well I'm glad that
your looking for a nice
jewish Dr. Just think,
a house in the country and
an apt. in the city, and
free drugs ... for the Whole
Family ... O.K.

Well its done, by the time
you read this letter, France
will be reading his. Oh well
mark that down for experience.

The summer's almost over and Big - B - here I come, I cann't wait.

The Van situation is a bit confussing, I think he's a bit lonely in N.Y. he really doesn't have that many friends and with Peter prancing around a constant reminder of that last year in Baltimore, which was a big mess, no wonder he's acting strange.

George isn't working anymore. I was in New York two week ends ago to see Van, and he (George) was in Ocean City with Glen - living off Richie & Sharon.

I had a real good time with Van in N.Y. We went to the movies to see "Midnight Cowboy," fantastic flick, and it was filmed in Van's neighborhood.

My cousin got married on Sun. in Long Island — very jewish affair — just like "Good Bye Columbus," wow lots of fun & lots to eat. From chicken Cow Mein to Bagel & Lox. Oh well this is just a small note to say hello, and to tell you that I wrote Lance. You will probably get a call from him

so tell him it's for the best etc.
get him to read the letter to you,
I think it's pretty good.

Oh well the star still shines
in the Great Eastern Megatopitos

Love,

Steve

P.S. If you talk to Ruby Real Dimond
tell her that she'll hear from
me soon.

P.SS. My phone is
1-215-258-0101

P.SSS. — your new
name — should be
★Venus — Goddess of
Love & Romance

O.K. Steve

Letter from Bonnie

Rembrandt Hotel
THURLOE PLACE, LONDON, S.W.7.
Telephone: KENsington 8100
Cables: Choicest, London S.W.7
Telex: 25071 (Reservations only)

DEAR JANET —

Cheerio sad greetings from London — home of kidney pies and messed-up currency systems!

How are you doing? And how is she doing?? I want you to feel honored, the only other person to get a letter is Freda.

Well — London is really a beautiful city, and the people aren't as cold as everyone says. It's just that they think all Americans are rich and stupid. But alot of people think I'm Canadian — for what its worth. So far I've been to the national gallery (very good) London museum (good) Piccadilly Circus, Windsor Castle, etc. etc. The guys here are gorgeous. Picked up a cute cab driver (not really) met a Spanish guy who looks alot like my old love Burt, (who stopped talking to me when I ignored his offer to go to his hotel with him) and a really cute waiter who likes American girls because they can speak the English language well (although the accents are awful, he said) & because American girls I can talk about other things besides "pop singers" — Obviously British girls are hung up on the Beatles still, & talk of nothing else. The mini-skirts are unbelievable — they barely

cover the rear end, and
everyone wears them. Are
going to Carnaby Street to shop
tomorrow —

Oh - also had my first
fight with Bert Gordon tonight
it was the first time we
were both sober and we both
got rude. explain everything
in detail when I get home.
Letters are no place for
stories —

Went to the opera tonight —
mmmmm tea — it's not my
cup of tea —

The only thing I regret is
not taking anything (!!!)
with me - this place would
be more amazing in that
condition...

After London were going to
Scotland & Ireland — so I'll
write from there.

Be good, give everyone my
love, and forgive me if
this letter makes no sense -
its about 4:30 A.M. and I
can't think —

LOVE (the star)
Boom

Another letter from Bonnie

Dear Janet -

Hi, dear! Thanks for your letter - its always good to hear from you, but especially when you write — you have such a literary flair!

I've been dating lately (Thanks to my sister's big mouth) She's been having all these weirdos call me. Tonight I had dinner with this guy who looked exactly like an old boyfriend of mine. (Eric) It was a nice dinner, but, oooh! this guy.

He must be an escaped sex pervert from somewhere. He asked me out for Sunday and cause I didn't know what else to say, I said yes. (dumb, dumb) I will definitely break it before then.

Then - I went out a few times with this rich boy - (really rich) and I really tried to like him (he has 2 Nikons) but it only goes to prove that money is not everything. He thinks he owns me - me, Ruby Pearl Diamond Boom-Boom! Imagine! I never realized how awful possessive men can be - I'll never hassle Jim again — if the problem comes up - Some other guys have been asking me out but after tonite I've decided to tell them that I've just become engaged.

Cannot wait until school starts —

I called you a few nights ago but you were asleep. I wanted to tell you about this job thing, but its ok because it fell through anyway. Gee, letters are nice

and all, but I'd much rather chet-chat! Can't wait until school starts! ———

How is your job? You keep looking for that one perfect Jewish doctor. He's looking for you, too, and will be tickled pink to find you! I really miss our talks - we have to get together soon!

Spoke to Bob - his mother is in the hospital. he might come to visit me - his vacation starts tomorrow for 2 weeks - I asked him why he didn't go to Greg's and he said " why would I want to go to Greg's?" Hmmm....

Well - do write back soon (love your letters) and, again, cannot wait until school starts!!! Love, Boom

Letter from George

Hi Bill

To hear from you was a joy! I love you.

My apologys for not corresponding, but, as you realize; life here on the Cape is so hectic. My summer has been — well I would say sensational. I have never felt a bit better physically or mentally. True, I was slaving like a demon — working 70 awful hours a six day week! Needless to say I had enough of that and quit when another establishment here offered me a job as a waiter. I am making good money and work on 3 6 hours a week. Van's visit was marvelous — I so hated to see him depart. He is, but you know all of that.

Everyone here is as I am. The movie was a roaring success — has been booked on a 17 city nationwide tour, John, Marina, and Venus de Ga Ga Kha are leaving Oct. 1 for Hollywood — tensil town, U. S. A. Howard and Ed are keeping there bayside residence for the winter. They too will probably take a months respite on the coast. The Lady Divine and myself may rent a lovely little cottage year-round. I would like to open my 30's Rainbow Room here. Its success you know, would be almost assured. Provincetown has become a year-round mecca for fun. The cast of characters is just so super — how can I tell you?

I miss you, Bonnie, Sharon and Richard down there — the idea of coming back to the city does nothing to me. I just can't get excited — So I don't know what I am going to do. I will decide soon.

Tell Boom to write — I love her — Kiss Kiss Kiss !!!

No matter what - I will be down to big B in mid to late September — I will look forward to seeing you and remember you have the most precious thing in the world . . .

My love
George

A Provincetown Letter from Howard

Sat.

Dear Stu,

Provincetown is glorious! I love being here. Opened a smart smoke shop of my very own. You ready? It's tiny, but good looking. I carry imported + domestic cigarettes, cigars, pipe tobacco, large assortment of sundries, paper flowers, hash pipes, roach holders, post cards, candy, gum + ugly sunglasses. I did all the decorating myself so you can imagine what the place looks like. Walls + accessories stained dark oak, trim in white + avacado. For lighting we used make-up mirror lights, so I look my best at all times. Wait till you see it. Luckily it's also situated facing Commercial. I'm busy cruising at all time. We're open six hrs a day, but I have a chick who works seven of them, which gives me loads of time for beach, parties, beach parties etc. I have just returned from a smart picnic at Mr. Melvin Scott's in the pines. I hope the rest of this letter makes sense, if you know what I mean.

The people here are "out of sight." I have met some really groovy ones. My hair is now Arlene Dahl red & looks stunning. I'm quite tan, & once again look like the ~~Starfaty~~ I really am. I run from photographers + newsmen all day. One must cope with these everyday hassels. Your outfit for your 10th year reunion sounds devroux. I must know it. Please tell me how to get in touch with Vax. Paul told me nothing of what happened, as I was too stoned to remember. And isn't there any ~~Dice~~ going on in that town. You mentioned only nice things. Let me know. Also, half the note you sent me was bitching. You've got fucking nerve. + plenty of time for "yachting with George + swimming with chick." Write more. Aside from my busy career with the studio; I am now an up + coming so to speak, + my time is as valuable as yours. So there! Huss! Some fucking Polish kid just knocked over my Indian. By the way, I have

a cigar store Indian outside. Stunning.
Everybody up here is fine. I'm living with
Dean & it's unreal. Have you spoken to
Barbara? I got a gay letter. David is a
Bouncer in a Dyke Bar. You ready? Jo Maples
and I have broken our engagement. I just
don't have the time right now. And I don't
have the strength right now to write any
more. Please write soon. & Come up. It's
heaven. I can't stand it. I'm stoned hung
on this gorgeous number from N.Y.C. Stunning.

P.S. Love to Peter,
George, Bonnie,
etc etc

Love, to Janet,
Galaxy Gruber

P.P.S. Do you love
this paper?

P.P.P.S. We got some of the greatest "A" I've had in a long
time. Let me know if you want

About the Author

Janet Freedman was born in Baltimore in 1945. She received a BFA in Painting from the Maryland Institute College of Art in 1970 and an MLA from Johns Hopkins University in 1999. Her first book "Kent Island the Land That Once Was Eden" began as her MLA graduate project and was published by The Maryland Historical Society Press in 2002. Her screenplay, *The Marlborough,* received a Governor's Citation and Maryland State Arts Council Individual Artist Award in 2007. A selection of her paintings, essays and reflections can be seen on her website: www.studioprose.com .

OTHER WORKS

KENT ISLAND: The Land That Once was Eden

Available through Amazon and other book sellers.

"Janet Freedman conducts a remarkably circumspect exploration of a place that engages all of the senses, including a heart that registers the passage of time into memory. This is no ordinary account, but a jewel of a book whose many facets reveal not only a fascinating, haunting place, but a creative inquiry imbued with imagination and grace"

Charles Camp, PhD

The Maryland Institute College of Art

MY WEBSITE

WWW.STUDIOPROSE.COM

I am an artist and author, and in each of these disciplines I share memories, tell stories, and present the impressions/emotions of my life experience. As a painter I am interested in the colors and textures of the natural world, the repeated patterns, the play of weather and light. Nature is not just what I see but what I feel. Books were a childhood sanctuary; the rhythms and patterns of the written word resonate with me; I am charmed and seduced by their ability to create place and mood, action and emotion on a page.

Endnotes

---

[i] McNatt, Glen "The Light Years of Landscapist Eugene Leake" The Baltimore Sun Arts Section, The Baltimore Sun 22 October 2000.

[ii] https://artbma.org/exhibitions/cone-collection

[iii] https://bcrp.baltimorecity.gov/parks/druid-hill

[iv] Fred Rasmussen "A Platter Full of Fond Connelly's Memories"; The Baltimore Sun 27 July, 2008

[v] Jacques Kelly "Diners fondly recall a cheap and tasty meal at Mee Jun Low Chinese restaurant"; The Baltimore Sun 22 January, 2019

[vi] https://en.wikipedia.org/wiki/Jacques_Maroger

[vii] https://en.wikipedia.org/wiki/Lithopane

[viii] https://baltimoreheritage.org/issue/emerson-mansion/

[ix] https://hub.jhu.edu/2014/09/22/john-waters-qa-hitchhiking

Printed in Great Britain
by Amazon

34595692R00109